narration and discourse in american realistic fiction

narration and discourse in american realistic fiction

JANET HOLMGREN McKAY

university of pennsylvania press

philadelphia 1982

Passages from The Norton Critical Edition of ADVENTURES OF
HUCKLEBERRY FINN, by Samuel Langhorne Clemens, edited by
Sculley Bradley, Richard Croom Beatty, E. Hudson Long, and
Thomas Cooley, are used with the permission of the publisher,
W. W. Norton & Company, Inc. Copyright © 1977, 1962, 1961, by
W. W. Norton & Company, Inc.

Quotations from W. D. Howells, THE RISE OF SILAS LAPHAM are
used by kind permission of Indiana University Press.

The tables on pp. 17, 19 are reproduced from Lubomir Doležel,
NARRATIVE MODES IN CZECH LITERATURE and are used with
permission of University of Toronto Press.

Library of Congress Cataloging in Publication Data

McKay, Janet Holmgren.
   Narration and discourse in American realistic fiction.

   Bibliography: p.
   Includes index.
   1. American fiction—19th century—History and criticism.
2. Realism in literature. 3. Narration (Rhetoric) 4. Direct discourse
in literature. 5. Indirect discourse in literature. I. Title.
PS374.R37M3   813'.009'12   82-4814
ISBN 0-8122-7844-5   AACR2

Printed in the United States of America

FOR DREW

contents

preface

The purpose of this study is to document the importance of narration and discourse in American realistic fiction and to offer, at the same time, a new approach to the analysis of narration and discourse through the language of the texts themselves. I am sure that readers will find, despite my best efforts, that they are troubled at times by the "reductive *géometrie* of linguistics," as Dorrit Cohn has called it. However, I hope that in illuminating the form of these texts I am not robbing them of their poetry. Unfortunately, like Mark Twain's river pilot ". . . when I had mastered the language of this water, I had made a valuable acquisition. But I had lost something, too." This is the trade-off of criticism, especially "linguistic" criticism. I would expect, though, that the writers in this study, conscious of style as they were, would have secretly appreciated this form of dissection for it digs into the intricacies of their language in order to admire it.

I could not have completed this study without the patient support and steadfast encouragement of my husband, Drew. My daughter, Elizabeth, arrived in its midst to create joyful confusion, and Vivian Fletcher helped us all sort it out. My parents cheered me on as did my sister, Beth Holmgren, who gave me many insights into formalist/Slavic criticism. Many friends and colleagues helped along the way. Foremost among them is my teacher and friend, William Howarth, who has continually affirmed the value of my research while helping me to improve my writing style. For helpful suggestions on methodology, analysis, and organization and for general encouragement, I thank Robert Brown, Jackson Bryer, Steve Cahir, George Dillon, E. L. Epstein, Caroline Karcher, Shirley Strum Kenny, Carla Peterson, Roger Shuy, Calhoun Winton, and Nancy Yanofsky. I also wish to thank John McGuigan, Acquisitions Editor for the University of Pennsylvania Press, for his responsiveness throughout the review process, and Wendy Steiner, who offered many insightful suggestions in her review for the press.

I am grateful to the National Endowment for the Humanities for a summer fellowship in 1978. Throughout the time that I was writing the book, the Library of Congress provided me with work space and access to its collection. Sally Glover, Ann Newton, and Dorothy Zachman, of the University of Maryland's English department, typed various portions of the manuscript ably and expeditiously, and Lisa McCullough helped me to prepare the final copy.

narration and discourse in american realistic fiction

1
accounting
for
voices

narrative modes

Accounting for narrative modes in fiction has become a preoccupation of current critical theory. The issue of narration builds on the fundamental distinction in fiction between the perspectives of the author and of his characters, and perhaps more significantly, on the degree to which the author overtly controls the characters in his story. The "implied" author[1] might narrate his story, in his own first-person voice or in the third-person voice of the traditional storyteller, or he might allow his characters to speak for themselves, even to the point of yielding primary responsibility for narration to one or more characters. This division between telling and showing, between mimesis and diegesis, is as old as critical theory. As Paul Hernadi notes, ". . . Socrates, in the third book of Plato's *Republic,* distinguished three modes of literary discourse, according to whether the poet, the characters, or poet and characters alternately speak."[2]

Yet another option emerges in the modern period: a char-

1. Wayne Booth's descriptive term for the "official scribe who writes in this manner," by contrast with the "real" author, will be used throughout this study (Wayne Booth, *Rhetoric of Fiction* [Chicago: University of Chicago Press, 1961], p. 71).

2. Paul Hernadi, *Beyond Genre: New Directions in Literary Classification* (Ithaca and London: Cornell University Press, 1972), p. 187.

3

acter may not "speak" for himself, but his perspective dominates the unfolding of the story. This "figural" orientation,[3] usually involving a Jamesian "central consciousness," enhances the significance of the narrative mode. As the narrator's role expands, the author's diminishes. If a story is to emerge dramatically or as the account of a single character or through the consciousnesses of various characters, then the presentation must somehow divorce narration from authorial control. In fact, an author can contrive to have his narrator misunderstand or misrepresent events or characters in a way that Wayne Booth has memorialized as "unreliable."[4]

The three novelists considered in this study, James, Howells, and Twain, experimented with new forms of storytelling. Over and above traditional considerations of setting, subject matter, and characterization, these three novelists are linked together by their preoccupation with narrative modes and characters' discourse. In fact, by redefining the role of the narrator, by foregrounding the voices of the characters, and by combining these two changes to present a variety of perspectives in the novels themselves, these writers created the "realistic" tradition and brought the American novel into the modern period. In order to understand their contribution to the shape of the novel, it is necessary to understand the complexities of narration and discourse and to have a means of accounting for narrative modes and of identifying characters' voices.

Critics have used the issue of perspective or point of view as the key to identifying types of narration and to separating narrator, author, and characters. The difficulty with this ap-

3. Franz Stanzel uses "figural" as a label for one narrative type in *Narrative Situations in the Novel: Tom Jones, Moby Dick, The Ambassadors, Ulysses,* trans. James P. Pusack (Bloomington: Indiana University Press, 1971).

4. Booth offers the following definition for this label: ". . . I have called a narrator *reliable* when he speaks for or acts in accordance with the norms of the work (which is to say, the implied author's norms), *unreliable* when he does not" (Booth, *Rhetoric of Fiction,* pp. 158–59).

proach lies in the widely divergent meanings assigned to point of view. It is vaguely and contradictorily defined or not defined at all by those who use it. Norman Friedman has attempted a systematic exploration of the relationship between point of view and narration. He explains that relationship in the following way:

> Since the problem of the narrator is adequate transmission of his story to the reader, the questions must be something like the following: (1) who talks to the reader? (author in third or first person, character in first, or ostensibly no one); (2) from what position regarding the story does he tell it? (above, periphery, center, front, or shifting); (3) what channels of information does the narrator use to convey the story to the reader? (author's words, thoughts, perceptions, feelings; or character's words and actions; or character's thoughts, perceptions, and feelings); and (4) at what distance does he place the reader from the story? (near, far, or shifting).[5]

Friedman's questions suggest that he sees point of view both in terms of voice, or mode of discourse, and perspective, or angle of vision. He goes on to present categories of narration, reflecting what Lubomir Doležel calls "anthropomorphic concepts and personifying terms (such as: 'omniscient' narrator, narrator with 'limited omniscience')."[6]

An approach like Friedman's runs into problems because the various planes, as Boris Uspensky calls them,[7] of point of view are not necessarily coincidental. Seymour Chatman insists that the term point of view can only be used to designate

---

5. Norman Friedman, *Form and Meaning in Fiction* (Athens: The University of Georgia Press, 1975), p. 142.

6. Lubomir Doležel, *Narrative Modes in Czech Literature* (Toronto and Buffalo: University of Toronto Press, 1973), p. 5.

7. Uspensky discusses the ideological, phraseological, spatial, and temporal plane and the plane of psychology in chapters 1 through 4 of *A Poetics of Composition: The Structure of the Artistic Text and Typology of a Compositional Form*, trans. V. Zavarin and S. Wittig (Berkeley and Los Angeles: University of California Press, 1973).

"the physical place or ideological situation or practical life-orientation to which narrative events stand in relation."[8] This definition derives from the fact that *the perspective and the expression need not be lodged in the same person.* His division parallels Gérard Genette's separation of the *perspective narrative* into *mode,* that is, "who sees," and *voix,* "who speaks."[9] This essential division raises doubts about the usefulness of "anthropomorphic" labels, which hopelessly confuse *mode* and *voix.* In fact, two different levels of literary study are involved in the division. On an analytical level, it is possible to find in the language of a text evidence of the responsibility for an utterance, and where that evidence is inconclusive, the language indicates, at the very least, the source of the ambiguity. This linguistic evidence can then be used to interpret the *mode* or perspective. Hernadi notes, "instead of asking, 'Who speaks?' we should try to clarify whose perceptions, thoughts, and feelings inform the world of a given work of literature."[10] In fact, however, it is not an either/or division. Identifying "who speaks" is a necessary preliminary to determining "who sees," and some way of characterizing the two poles of point of view must obtain for this crucial distinction to be applied to the analysis of fiction.

In the analyses of narration and discourse in this study, I have used an analytical framework modeled after Doležel's with modifications to suit the texts and to reflect other compatible approaches. Doležel's approach differs from the standard models in two important ways. He bases his categories of narration (narrative modes) on discourse types that are

---

8. Seymour Chatman, *Story and Discourse: Narrative Structure of Fiction and Film* (Ithaca and London: Cornell University Press, 1978), p. 153.

9. "Toutefois, la plupart des travaux théoretiques sur ce sujet (qui sont essentiellement des classifications) souffrent à mon sens d'une fâcheuse confusion entre ce que j'appelle ici *mode* et *voix,* c'est-à-dire entre la question *quel est le personnage dont le point de vue oriente la perspective narrative?* et cette question tout autre: *qui est le narrateur?*—ou, pour parler plus vite, entre la question *qui voit?* et la question *qui parle?*" (Gérard Genette, *Figures III* [Paris: Seuil, 1972], p. 203).

10. Hernadi, *Beyond Genre,* p. 188.

determined by the presence or absence of certain linguistic features. His modes, which are equivalent to narrative perspectives, are then, only minimally "anthropomorphic." He divides first- and third-person narration into three subcategories: personal *Ich*-form, observer's *Ich*-form, rhetorical *Ich*-form; subjective *Er*-form, objective *Er*-form, rhetorical *Er*-form. The objective or observer category involves the narrator in representation only; the rhetorical allows him representation and interpretation; and the subjective or personal adds involvement in the action to the other two functions. These categories, in and of themselves, while novel, are not the most distinguishing feature of Doležel's approach. He uses textual features, involving pronominal reference, tense marking, phonological idiosyncrasies, etc., to identify the categories. Therefore, his approach incorporates a two-step procedure moving from voice to perspective. A number of other critical methodologies, including those of Chatman, Genette and Dorrit Cohn, adopt an approach similar to Doležel's, but his seems to me the most explicit and systematic.

Chatman and Cohn have categories that coincide with a number of distinctions I make throughout. Chatman approaches narration largely through voice: "It is less important to categorize types of narrators than to identify the features that mark their degrees of audibility. A quantitative effect applies: the more identifying features, the stronger our sense of a narrator's presence."[11] The features he uses to determine "audibility" are similar to Doležel's although less systematically presented. Doležel uses linguistic features to identify discourse types that in turn determine narrative modes, while Chatman starts with discourse types and moves to perspectives—a minor difference. Chatman develops one particularly noteworthy dichotomy. His narrative types move from covert to overt narrator. The covert category encompasses the "anti-

11. Chatman, *Story and Discourse*, p. 196.

omniscient"[12] tendencies of the narrators discussed in this study; the overt narrator demonstrates some degree of intrusiveness. The covert/overt rather than the first/third-person axis is fundamental to Chatman's discussion—an improvement on other approaches because it allows for the shift from first to third person in narrative voice so common in fiction of all periods. Chatman offers, for his overt narrators, types of involvement—interpretation, judgment, generalization—similar to Doležel's subcategories of *Ich* and *Er* forms. Finally, both theories permit a range of narrative functions in any given text. As Chatman notes, "even in *The Ambassadors,* where narration is strongly covert, the narrator makes an occasional interpretation."[13]

Cohn's study focuses specifically on the narration of characters' thoughts. She makes a very important distinction between indirectly quoted thought and " 'other mind stuff' (as William James called it) . . . [that] can only be narrated."[14] Cohn labels this "stuff" "the nonverbal realm of consciousness." Henry James, and occasionally Howells, uses narrative description ("psycho-narration" as Cohn calls it) to explain a character's knowledge or feeling that does not take the form of inner speech. The narrator's language "is meant to elucidate rather than emulate the figural psyche."[15] However, unlike more modern writers, such as Joyce, none of the authors included in this study attempted to articulate these thought-patterns in nonverbal forms. They were not interested in thought divorced from a speech model. Thus, in this study the term *discourse* will include both actual speech forms and "verbalized" thoughts.

Cohn assumes a basic first/third-person distinction in nar-

---

12. I will use this term, coined by Harold Kolb, Jr., *The Illusion of Life: American Realism as a Literary Form* (Charlottesville: The University Press of Virginia, 1969), p. 64, throughout this study to designate narrators who pointedly disclaim any pretense of omniscience.

13. Chatman, *Story and Discourse,* p. 240.

14. Dorrit Cohn, *Transparent Minds: Narrative Modes for Presenting Consciousness in Fiction* (Princeton: Princeton University Press, 1978), p. 11.

15. Ibid., p. 55.

rative modes. Within each person, however, she uses labels that reflect a discourse base, and she identifies the relationship between narrating voice and "the consciousness he narrates"[16] as either "dissonant" (distanced) or "consonant" (fused).[17] In both her first- and third-person modes, she reserves a role for the narrator, who can "tell"—"psycho-narration," "self-narration," or allow characters to tell—"quoted monologue," "self-quoted monologue," or intervene minimally—"narrated monologue," "self-narrated monologue." Her final category, "autonomous monologue," is the only one in which the narrator seems to disappear.

Disappearing or nonexistent narrators are the subject of much current study. Focus on narration has resulted in a tendency for critics to see an ever increasing number of narrators in individual texts. Several theorists have taken a stand against this proliferation by positing the category "narratorless." For such linguistically oriented critics as Ann Banfield and S.-Y. Kuroda,[18] this type derives from their identification of certain discourse types as "speakerless." Donald Ross comes at the issue through perspective rather than voice by suggesting that the narrative function can be "attributed" to

16. Ibid., p. 26.

17. Cohn notes that her polarity corresponds to Stanzel's authorial-figural distinction and "to a whole series of polarities proposed by other critics: *vision per derrière-vision avec* (Pouillon, Todorov), telling-showing (Booth), non-focalized-focalized (Genette) etc." (Cohn, *Transparent Minds*, p. 275).

18. Ann Banfield, "Narrative Style and the Grammar of Direct and Indirect Speech," *Foundations of Language* 10 (1973): 1–39, and "The Formal Coherence of Represented Speech and Thought," *Poetics and Theory of Literature* 3 (1978): 289–314; S.-Y. Kuroda, "Where Epistemology, Style, and Grammar Meet: A Case Study from Japanese," in *A Festschrift for Morris Halle*, ed. Stephen R. Anderson and Paul Kiparsky (New York: Holt, Rinehart & Winston, 1973), pp. 377–91, and "Reflections on the Foundations of Narrative Theory: From a Linguistic Point of View," in *Pragmatics of Language and Literature*, ed. Teun A. van Dijk (Amsterdam: North-Holland Publishing Company, 1976), pp. 107–40. Both Banfield and Kuroda relate their "speakerless/narratorless" argument to that of Käte Hamburger, *The Logic of Literature*, trans. Marilynn J. Ross (Bloomington and London: Indiana University Press, 1973), who finds a personalized narrator only in first-person novels. She identifies a "narrative function" in third-person texts; this function for Hamburger does not involve an actual narrator.

a character in the story.[19] In both theories, free indirect discourse, discussed below, plays a significant role. In general, the arguments for "narratorless" involve an oversimplification of the narrative function and an insufficient awareness of the distinction between *mode* and *voix*. To say, as Banfield does, that a narrator exists only when information is present in a story that no character can know is to require every narrator to fulfill the traditional omniscient storytelling role.[20] In turn, attributing narration to the author or character imposes unnecessary limitations on the narrative voice. For example, Ross says of *The Ambassadors* that "attributing the [first] paragraph (and most of the novel) to Strether as a source greatly simplifies the explanation and removes the need to search for a ghostly narrator who is sometimes external to the events and characters."[21] Had James wanted Strether "to talk" throughout the novel, he could have written it in the first person without the narrative device of distancing that his limited third-person approach permits. Moreover, the narrator in the paragraph is far from "ghostly." As Ross notes, "the only problem with the tidy picture is the story-teller's clause, 'I have just mentioned.' While this does introduce an explicit speaker different from Strether, I question whether it is substantial or personal, or just part of the mechanics of relating the story."[22] A narrator need not have a "substantial" existence or a personality to exercise the narrative function, and it would seem that "the mechanics of relating the story" is, in fact, a good definition of the narrative function.

19. Donald Ross, Jr., "Who's Talking? How Characters Become Narrators in Fiction," *Modern Language Notes* 91 (1976): 1222–42. In this study, I will use "attributable to" in the sense of "interpreted as the responsibility of." Ross uses the term "attribute" much more generally, describing the process of "attribution" as follows: "An *attributing* clause, which tells who talks or thinks, labels the activity in the predicate, and optionally tells how the activity is delivered: 'said Pauline, looking up' and 'whispering, however, with gravity' " (p. 1225).

20. Banfield, "Formal Coherence of Speech and Thought," p. 299.

21. Ross, "Who's Talking?" p. 1232.

22. Ibid., p. 1233.

My own approach to the question of the narrator's presence coincides with Doležel's and Chatman's. Doležel starts from the position that all forms of discourse other than directly reported discourse are the narrator's responsibility. One might say that a narrative "I," not necessarily a personality, controls narrative discourse,[23] but the responsibility for the linguistic elements of that discourse can be ambiguous or transferred. Chatman refers to stories with the most covert of narrators as being " 'non'-or minimally narrated."[24] He makes a further important distinction between the author, the "implied" author, and the narrator. Even in a context where the author connects the speaking voice of the text specifically with himself, "the speaker is not the author, but, the 'author' (quotation marks of 'as if'), or better the 'author-narrator,' one of several possible kinds."[25] In other words, the author becomes a type of narrator. Moreover, the "implied" author is "not the narrator, but rather the principle that invented the narrator, along with everything else in the narrative. . . ."[26] The "implied" author creates the narrator, who, or less personally, which is the voice in the text that speaks to the reader. This voice is Doležel's DN (narrator's discourse) and it mingles with the characters' voices when the narrator records those voices indirectly.

discourse types

If we approach narration through discourse, we can determine responsibility for perspective only after we have as-

---

23. This position on narration is roughly analogous to the performative linguistic theory that posits an "I" plus a performative verb (e.g., *assert*) before every utterance. See, for example, J. R. Ross, "On Declarative Sentences," in *Readings in English Transformational Grammar*, ed. R. A. Jacobs and P. S. Rosenbaum (Waltham, Mass.: Ginn, 1970), pp. 222–72.

24. Chatman, *Story and Discourse*, p. 196.

25. Ibid., p. 148.

26. Ibid.

signed responsibility for utterances themselves. Linguists recognize two types of discourse in naturally occurring speech: direct and indirect. In literature, we find a third type—free indirect—that combines features of direct and indirect. In direct discourse, responsibility for an utterance is a straightforward matter. Whether I say, "in my opinion, Jimmy Carter was a good president," or simply, "Jimmy Carter was a good president," the utterance, including the evaluative *good,* is my responsibility. I need not believe what I say nor need it be true. Depending on such variables as intonation and paralingual signals, I can make my utterance sarcastic, doubting, and so forth. Nevertheless, because it is direct discourse, I am responsible for it. This pattern of responsibility applies to directly *reported* discourse as well. As both Barbara Hall Partee and Ann Banfield have shown, in a construction such as "Harry said, 'Reagan is a good president,' " there are two speakers, the reporting "I" and "Harry."[27] The reported sentence is Harry's responsibility, while the introductory clause is the responsibility of the speaker, "I." When we move from directly reported to indirectly reported discourse, the responsibility becomes less clear.

Partee and Banfield have demonstrated that indirectly quoted forms in naturally occurring speech cannot be derived from the similar direct quotation. For example, in (1) it is not at all clear what "he" said:

1. He said my accent reminds him of you.

The statement may be an indirect rendering of "Your accent reminds me of X," or it may be a summary of any number of other direct forms, e.g., "You talk as weirdly as X does." Given this analysis, it would be logical to assume that in all indirectly reported speech, the speaker of the entire utterance

27. See Banfield, "Narrative Style," p. 20, and Barbara Hall Partee, "The Syntax and Semantics of Quotation," in *A Festschrift for Morris Halle,* ed. Stephen R. Anderson and Paul Kiparsky (New York: Holt, Rinehart & Winston, 1973), pp. 412–30.

is responsible for all elements in it, including evaluative words, such as *stupid* in (2):

2. Harry said his stupid brother is coming to town.

Banfield asserts that because of the nonderived relationship between directly and indirectly reported speech, this type of sentence can only be given what philosophers label a *de re*, or as Tanya Reinhart calls it, a transparent reading[28]—the *stupid* (as well as everything else) is attributable to the speaker of the sentence and not to Harry since we can never know exactly what Harry said. As Banfield maintains: "Any expressive words and constructions in indirect speech always express the state and attitude of the speaker who reports it."[29]

Although this "speaker-coherence" argument, as Dillon and Kirchhoff call it,[30] seems logical in terms of linguistic consistency, it must be questioned on pragmatic grounds. Most speakers, confronted with the sentence out of context, would assume that the reported clause, although indirect, still includes Harry's words. Moreover, a sentence such as (3) seems to encourage the assumption that Harry is responsible for the reported clause.

3. His stupid brother is coming to town, Harry said.

However, contexts can be constructed that shift responsibility for the reported clause to the speaker giving the report. The simplest way to prompt a speaker-oriented interpretation is to stress *stupid*. Another method involves the discourse itself. Thus a construction like "I think Harry's brother is an idiot, and Harry says his stupid brother is coming to town"

28. Tanya Reinhart, "Whose Main Clause? (Point of View in Sentences with Parentheticals)," *Harvard Studies in Syntax and Semantics,* ed. S. Kuno (Cambridge: Department of Linguistics, Harvard University, 1975) 1: 128.

29. Banfield, "Narrative Style," p. 21.

30. George Dillon and Frederick Kirchhoff, "On the Form and Function of Free Indirect Style," *Poetics and Theory of Literature* 1 (1976): 431.

suggests that the reporting speaker is also offering the evaluation.

Conclusions about whether an indirectly reported form contains features attributable to the embedded speaker involve many considerations other than the few contextual and linguistic variables I have indicated. The hearer has to evaluate what he knows of the relationship between the reporting and the reported speaker, the general reliability of the reporting speaker, the reporting and reported speakers' attitudes toward the situation being described, and so forth. These "extralinguistic contextual features"[31] are crucial to assigning responsibility. Of course, the hearer always has recourse to a direct question about responsibility. Unfortunately, this recourse is not available to the reader of a newspaper account containing reported assertions, nor to hearer/readers in a variety of other settings. The most extreme case of nonrecoverability involves indirectly reported speech in literature because there is usually no direct antecedent for the fictitious indirect report. As Brian McHale notes: ". . . in fiction . . . there is no direct 'original' prior to or behind an instance of ID [indirect discourse] or FID [free indirect discourse]; the supposedly 'derived' utterances are not versions of anything, but are themselves the 'originals' in that they give as much as the reader will ever learn of 'what was really said.' "[32]

Despite the fact that indirectly reported speech in literature usually lacks an antecedent, studies of discourse types involving literary interpretation usually assume that indirect reports closely resemble their hypothetical direct antecedents. Donald Ross says: "Indirect quotation implies that the character's actual words could be found if quotation marks were put in and some changes made in pronouns and verb tenses, as in *He said that he did* → *He said, 'I do.'* "[33] This derivational rela-

31. Robin Lakoff, "Language in Context," *Language* 48 (1972): 926.
32. Brian McHale, "Free Indirect Discourse: A Survey of Recent Accounts," *Poetics and Theory of Literature* 3 (1978): 256.
33. Ross, "Who's Talking?" p. 1223.

tionship also underlies Chatman's paradigm for methods of reporting speech and thought:

	Tagged	Free
Direct:		
Speech	"I have to go," she said	I have to go
Thought	"I have to go," she thought	I have to go

	Tagged	Free
Indirect:		
Speech	She said that she had to go	She had to go
Thought	She thought that she had to go	She had to go[34]

Richard Ohmann's early transformational model to account for free indirect discourse was also based on a derivational pattern linking direct, indirect, and free indirect reporting.[35]

In light of the Banfield/Partee analysis it is clearly an overgeneralization to assume a derivational relationship between direct discourse and the indirect report of it, although in ordinary language use this relationship seems to account for at least one possible interpretation of responsibility. In this sense readers of literature model their response on their experiences with nonliterary language as McHale describes them: "In everyday production and use of represented/reported discourse, it is theoretically always possible to recover the 'original' direct utterance from the derived nondirect versions, or at least to think of it as recoverable, 'basic' to the non-direct transforms."[36]

The examples we have looked at thus far are of the embed-

34. Chatman, *Story and Discourse*, p. 201.

35. Richard Ohmann, "Generative Grammars and the Concept of Literature," *Word* 20 (1964): 435.

36. McHale, "Free Indirect Discourse," p. 256.

ded clause form, involving a verb of communication *(verbum dicendi)* with or without the subordinator *that.* The fact that they are open to more than one interpretation leads to Reinhart's conclusion: ". . . complex sentences of saying and believing . . . are essentially ambiguous with respect to who said/believed what."[37] I would add the proviso that they are far less likely to be ambiguous in context. Sentences need not be complex, however, to report a speech act. Forms such as (4) cannot be given "derivational" interpretations of the type suggested by Ross but still hold the possibility of confusion about who is responsible for the reported portion:

4. Harry told me to thank his stupid brother.

While (4) seems likely to have a speaker-oriented interpretation, a similar sentence (5) seems more Harry-oriented.

5. Harry asked me to thank his stupid brother for him.

This more oblique reporting method is frequent in literature. Ross notes that in paraphrase sometimes ". . . a hint of the actual [reported] words shows through. . . ."[38] This is also the case in McHale's "summary, less 'purely' diegetic; summary which to some degree represents, not merely gives notice of, a speech event. . . ."[39]

In short, every example of indirectly reported speech, no matter how it is reported, seems to have the *potential* of including elements that are the responsibility of the embedded speaker, and this possibility is often deliberately exploited in literature. As Doležel says: "discourse ambiguity seems to be an inherent property of the narrative text structure, resulting from the dynamic character of the opposition DN [narrator's discourse]—DC [characters' discourse]."[40] This potential

37. Reinhart, "Whose Main Clause?" p. 130.
38. Ross, "Who's Talking?" p. 1223.
39. McHale, "Free Indirect Discourse," p. 259.
40. Doležel, *Narrative Modes*, p. 12.

ambiguity in both everyday and literary language proves the "speaker-coherence" approach to be too rigid. Moreover, this model presents particular problems in its analysis of free indirect discourse (FID).

FID is the most complex method of mixing directly and indirectly reported discourse. There is considerable variation in labeling this form, but its basic characteristics are generally agreed upon.[41] As Dillon and Kirchhoff assert:

> In general, the material that appears in FIS [free indirect style] is to be understood as a representation of a character's expressions or thoughts as he would express them . . . Thus, although the pronouns referring to the character are third-person, not first, and the tense (usually) 'backshifted' from the tense the character would use, in other respects the material is given as he would assign it rather than as the narrator would.[42]

Apart from verb tense and pronominal forms this discourse type is as close to direct discourse as an indirect form can be—a fact that prompts Charles Fillmore to say: "In represented speech it is nearly possible to represent his [the reported speaker's] exact words; but in reported speech it is not."[43]

FID, unlike other indirectly reported discourse, admits exclamations, broken sentences (elliptical or fragmented forms), and an unusual distribution of sentence patterns, such as subject-auxiliary inversion in questions, usually restricted to sentences that cannot follow an introductory phrase (he said that . . .). So, for example, constructions occur as in (6)

41. In French criticism it is commonly called *style indirect libre*, in German *erlebte Rede*. McHale lists a number of its labels in English (McHale, "Free Indirect Discourse," pp. 1–2, fn. 1). I will follow McHale in using the label free indirect discourse, which identifies this as a formal method for reporting discourse, like direct and indirect, rather than characterizing it as a literary style.

42. Dillon and Kirchhoff, "Free Indirect Style," p. 431.

43. "Pragmatics and the Description of Discourse," *Berkeley Studies in Syntax and Semantics*, ed. C. Fillmore, G. Lakoff, R. Lakoff (Berkeley: Dept. of Linguistics and Institute of Human Learning, University of California, 1974) 1: V–11.

and (7). The characters address themselves or some unspecified audience, but do not speak directly in the first person.

> 6. Was he the sort of man to be allowed to play her false with impunity?
>
> W. D. Howells, *The Rise of Silas Lapham*[44]
>
> 7. That was years before, when this girl must have been a child; but hadn't it thrown a kind of rainbow over her cradle and wouldn't she naturally have some gift?
>
> Henry James, *The Bostonians*[45]

If FID is so similar to directly reported discourse, then it should be relatively easy to identify responsibility for the language of FID. It should be, as Fillmore suggests, that of the reported speaker. The expressions of FID are not uttered directly by the reported speaker, but they appear to represent that speaker's judgments. The problem, of course, is that these are not direct discourse forms and because they have some features in common with indirectly reported forms, they should be open to the ambiguous interpretation of all ID.

In order to free FID from the restrictive *de re* interpretations of indirect forms, Banfield, following Kuroda's lead, argues that FID is a "speakerless" phenomenon—the presentation of a perspective outside the normal communication paradigm that usually characterizes language. This analysis is based on the fact that many examples of FID cannot be derived from tagged indirect forms (John said that he would be going) precisely because of the features FID has in common with directly reported discourse.

The concept of a "speakerless" style is an interesting one;

44. William Dean Howells, *The Rise of Silas Lapham*, intro. and notes to the Text by Walter J. Meserve, Text established by Walter J. Meserve and David J. Nordloh (Bloomington and London: Indiana University Press, 1971), p. 338. The passage that includes this sentence is discussed in chapter 3, pp. 132–33, of this book.

45. Henry James, *The Bostonians*, ed. with intro. by Irving Howe (New York: The Modern Library, Random House, 1956), p. 38. The passage that includes this sentence is discussed in chapter 2, p. 65 of this book.

the label reflects in large part what writers using FID attempt to convey—consciousness without the obvious intervention of a narrative voice. However, the Kuroda/Banfield argument is open to criticism on several counts. First, it ignores the functions of the discourse form. FID can convey either ironic distance or empathy/sympathy. Certainly, writers seem to choose it over directly and indirectly reported discourse because of its subtlety in expressing these relationships. To account for both irony and empathy we have to posit two speakers or as McHale says, "... when FID functions as vehicle of irony or empathy there are at least two sources, often difficult to distinguish: the character whose utterance is being reported and also an author/narrator who intervenes somehow, to some degree, in the report and is responsible for the irony or sympathy itself."[46]

Secondly, Reinhart offers a syntactic solution to the absence of a controlling clause, and thus of a speaker, in FID. She speculates that an underlying parenthetical (he said, etc.) controls sequences of FID. A parenthetical would follow rather than precede the sequences in question, and thus avoid the problem of embedding.[47] If a parenthetical following FID

46. McHale, "Free Indirect Discourse," pp. 278–79.

47. FID sentences would then be equivalent to Reinhart's subject-oriented sentences containing parentheticals (SCP's). Sentence (1) is a subject-oriented SCP, the main clause reflects Ed's point of view, and contrasts with (2), a speaker-oriented SCP, in which the main clause reflects the point of view of the speaker of the entire utterance:

    1. He $_i$ would be late, Ed $_i$ said.
    2. Ed $_i$ will be late, he $_i$ said. (Reinhart, "Whose Main Clause?" p. 143)

The tense agreement between the main clause and the parenthetical, the backward pronominalization (obligatory in subject-oriented SCP's), and the intonation pattern ("like a direct quote followed by a parenthetical") (Reinhart, "Whose Main Clause?" p. 143) all make (1) subject-oriented. In (2), by contrast, the parenthetical functions like a sentence adverbial to qualify or emphasize the speaker's report about Ed and not like the tag of directly reported discourse. For Banfield, these parentheticals do not contradict the "speakerless" designation of FID because they are derived in her analysis so as to be unable to include expressive elements (the only evidence in her model for point of view). Thus a sentence (3) is not "so acceptable" because of the expressive *mistakenly* (Banfield, "Formal Coherence of Speech and Thought," p. 305).

forms argues against the "speakerless" explanation, then a far more devastating attack would be involved if FID forms could be embedded, that is, preceded by a *verbum dicendi* plus a subordinating *that*. A sentence like (8) would be an example of an embedded exclamation form:

> 8. Jim said he bet she did think of it . . . and he believed they must a gone up town to get a dog . . . or else we wouldn't be here on a tow-head . . .—no, indeedy, we would be in that same old town. . . .
>
> Mark Twain, *Adventures of Huckleberry Finn* [48]

Banfield does indicate that some instances of FID can be introduced by verbs of communication,[49] but this pattern would presumably not extend to constructions, like exclamations or interjections, that cannot ordinarily be reported indirectly.[50]

---

3. ?He was more in love with her than she had supposed, Emma mistakenly { thought
{ supposed.

This argument is not convincing, first, because (3) does not seem particularly unacceptable, especially if it were placed in context, and second, because many sentences like (3) come to mind that are completely acceptable:

4. He ᵢ would be late, Ed ᵢ tactlessly said.
5. He ᵢ wouldn't be put upon any longer, Ed ᵢ cried angrily.
6. No, the work wasn't hard, Mary responded cheerfully.

It is somewhat more difficult to introduce evaluative words into the parentheticals of FID than it is in the tags of direct discourse, a fact which suggests once again that while these forms resemble direct discourse, they are not identical to it. More interesting, though, is the question of whose point of view is represented in the evaluative words of the parenthetical. It seems that they are most often the responsibility of the reporting speaker (although not always) rather than of the parenthetical subject.

48. Samuel Langhorne Clemens, *Adventures of Huckleberry Finn: An Authoritative Text, Backgrounds and Sources, Criticism*, ed. Sculley Bradley, Richmond Croom Beatty, E. Hudson Long, Thomas Cooley (New York: W. W. Norton & Company, Inc., 1977), p. 55.

49. Banfield, "Narrative Style," p. 30.

50. The problem with the general argument of nonembeddability, which then eliminates the "speaker" of the sentence, is that what is and what is not embeddable is far from resolved. Georgia Green ("Main Clause Phenomena in Subordinate Clauses," *Language* 52, 1976) in discussing main clause phenomena—"certain constructions fully grammatical in main clauses, but odd or ungrammatical—in any case,

Thus, although certain instances of FID, constructions without the parenthetical tag and with many direct discourse features, encourage a "univocal"[51] or "speakerless" interpretation, the discourse type itself must be seen as basically "narrated." Cohn explains this relationship in justifying the adaptation of the term "narrated monologue" for FID:

> To speak only of a *dual* presence . . . seems to me misleading: for the effect of the narrated monologue is precisely to reduce to the greatest degree the hiatus between the narrator and the figure existing in all third-person narration. But to speak simply of a *single* presence . . . is even more misleading: for one then risks losing sight of the difference between third-and first-person narration . . . In narrated monologues, as in figural narration generally, the continued employment of third-person references indicates, no matter how unobtrusively, the continued presence of the narrator.[52]

Finally, given the specific features of FID, the number of sentences of this type is necessarily quite small. FID is rarely used exclusively or even consistently in long stretches. Rather it alternates with other more traditional forms of narration.

In Doležel's model, as illustrated in Table 1, characters' discourse (DC), which manifests itself as direct discourse (DD), and narrative commentary (DN) represent extremes in terms of the seven textual features that explain discourse types. (1) In terms of the system of grammatical persons, DC has a three-person system, while DN has only one—the third person;[53] however, "DN of the *Ich*-form is characterized by a two-person system: the first person, referring to the *Ich*-narrator,

---

much less acceptable—in embedded clauses" (pp. 382-3), concludes that ". . . the principles determining the embeddability of so-called MCP are pragmatic and conversational, and not formal or syntactic at all" (p. 386).

51. McHale, "Free Indirect Discourse," p. 279.

52. Cohn, *Transparent Minds*, p. 112.

53. Doležel, *Narrative Modes*, p. 21.

Table 1[54]

Mode of Characters' Speech	Discrim-inative Features	system of persons	system of tenses	deixis	allocu-tion	emotive function	subjective semantics	specified speech level
DN	o	o	o	o	o	o	o	o
RD	o	o/1	1	1*	1	1	1	1
DC	1	1	1	1	1	1	1	1

(*with formal modifications)

and the third person, relating the action to the referent (to the 'narrated events')."[55] (2) In DN the basic verbal tense is past; in DC ". . . tense expresses the reference to the individual and the shifting time position of the speaker, the speaking character."[56] (3) Deixis (time and space adverbs, *here/now*, demonstrative pronouns *this/that*) in DC is controlled "by the time and space position of its speaker-character";[57] in DN "demonstrative means . . . point to some spatial or temporal centres of the narrated action. . . ."[58] (4) "The allocutional function [relationship to hearer] in DC is expressed by certain allocutional means, the most important of which in Czech are imperative mood, interrogative sentence and the vocative case as a means of address . . . DN has no allocutional function inasmuch as it is, by definition, utterance without hearer."[59] (5) The emotive function (expressing the speaker's attitude toward his subject) is absent from DN, but interjections, exclamations, etc. are typical of DC.[60] (6) Semantic features (expressing opinion or mood of the speaker other than those

54. Ibid., p. 41.
55. Ibid., p. 23. This explanation of the DN of the *Ich*-form does not account for a colloquial narrator, like Huck Finn, who addresses the reader directly in the second person.
56. Ibid., p. 26.
57. Ibid., p. 28.
58. Ibid., p. 29.
59. Ibid., p. 30.
60. Ibid., p. 33.

covered by the emotive function) are absent from DN and characteristic of DC.[61] (7) Speech-level features, "verbal means reflecting the speaker's idiolect," are likewise absent from DN and characteristic of DC.[62]

By definition, then, and as illustrated in Table 2 from Doležel, categories 4, 5, 6, and to a certain extent 3 and 7, equate DN with the "objective *Er*-form," which is equivalent to Banfield's "narrative exposition"[63] and to Chatman's "non- or minimally narrated." The first-person counterpart to the objective *Er*-form, the "observer's *Ich*-form," demonstrates DC features in only 1 and 2. The narrative mode labeled "rhetorical *Er*-form" demonstrates some evidence of

Table 2[64]

Narrative Mode	Text Features	system of persons	system of tenses	deixis	allocution	emotive function	subjective semantics	specified speech level
personal *Ich*-form		1^a	1^a	1^a	1^a	1^a	1^a	1^a
subjective *Er*-form		o	o	$1^a/o$	$1^a/o$	$1^a/o$	$1^a/o$	$1^a/o$
objective *Er*-form		o	o	o	o	o	o	o
rhetorical *Er*-form		o	o	1	1	1	1	1
observer's *Ich*-form		1	1	o	o	o	o	o
rhetorical *Ich*-form		1	1	1	1	1	1	1

61. Ibid., p. 34. This category includes "attitudinal semantics," which "employs qualifying adjectives and adverbs, carrying the speaker's evaluation of an object or action" (p. 35) and "subjective modality" in which "the modal status of verbal actions is . . . controlled by the decision of a speaker, in accordance with the general trends of his subjective semantics" (p. 37). Doležel's "attitudinal semantics" is equivalent to Banfield's "evaluative words."

62. Ibid., p. 39.

63. Banfield, "Formal Coherence of Speech and Thought," p. 296.

64. Doležel, *Narrative Modes*, p. 10.

DC in categories 3 and 7, as does the "subjective *Er-*form," but in the latter the features are further distinguished by the fact that the narrator is involved in the action. A "rhetorical *Ich-*form" has DC features in all seven categories, as does a "personal *Ich*-form," in which the narrator is involved in the action.

Represented discourse (RD), Doležel's label for ID, shares the textual features of DN for the first two categories and some DC features in categories 3–7. But Doležel makes an important distinction between *compact* and *diffused* RD:

> If the density of these features [3–7] is sufficiently high, a compact and unambiguous form of RD arises. If the positive features are dispersed thinly, as sporadic signals on the DN base, the result is just a "tinge" of DN; an ambiguous portion of text arises which blends positive signals with negative signals. In our frame of reference, this device could be called *diffused* RD.[65]

In other words, Doležel's RD covers the whole range of reported forms from McHale's "diegetic summary" to what is traditionally labeled FID (compact RD). His definition of compact RD hinges on the accumulation of DC features.[66]

Doležel's model demonstrates how the presentation of discourse can signal the degree of narrator presence in a given

---

65. Ibid., p. 51. If my reading of this relationship is correct, then "a 'tinge' of DN" should read "a 'tinge' of DC" since there should be more DN where the features are thinly distributed. I have chosen to use the label ID (indirectly reported discourse) rather than RD throughout this study because of the apposition of ID with DD and because it occurs more consistently in studies of literary discourse.

66. If compact ID, or FID, is taken to be primarily a syntactic operation, i.e., a question of embeddability, we would have to rank Doležel's features, giving greater weight to a feature like "allocutional" than to one like "subjective semantics." I see no reason for this arbitrary distinction between syntax and semantics because I think the preponderance of features rather than the nature of the feature *per se* must be the deciding factor. However, writers using FID usually dissociate it from diffused RD by dropping the introductory *verbum dicendi.* Perhaps a distinction should be made between "nonembeddable"—those syntactic forms which apparently cannot follow a verb of saying—and "nonembedded," a surface/contextual phenomenon, the former offering a slightly greater indication of the character's voice.

expression. He diagrams the "dynamic relationship between DN and DC" as follows:

DN→ discourse NC (diffused RD)→ RD (compact RD)→ DC[67]

This diagram captures the relatively close relationship of compact RD to direct discourse as well as the somewhat more distant relationship of directly and indirectly reported forms. At the same time, it shows the merging of narrator and character voices as we move away from DN. It successfully integrates discourse types with narrative function and allows linguistic features to account for voice to the degree that this is possible. Finally, Doležel's model offers us a way to analyze the dynamic tension between narrator and character voices in a novel. Such an analysis is fundamental to the exploration of the somewhat vague category of "realism," for the concept of realism derives as much from how a story is presented as from what is presented in the story.

american literary realism

Realism is to literary typology what point of view is to narrative typology: an elusive and loosely defined category that critics use authoritatively because they assume a commonality of understanding.[68] Harold Kolb, addressing the tradition within American literature, notes that common definitions of realism "depend on a small, often-repeated group of singularly evasive words—'truth,' 'actuality,' 'accuracy,'

---

67. Doležel, *Narrative Modes*, p. 53. NC appears to represent a blend of narrator/character voices.

68. As Harold Kolb notes, "the term 'realism' has a remarkable vogue, although its popularity seems to be inversely proportional to the precision with which it has been used" (Kolb, *Illusion of Life*, p. 11). On the other hand, Marshall Brown points out the importance of the label: "The seeming endlessness of the debate argues for the complexity of the term, not for its meaninglessness. To review what has been said about realism is thus to encounter a series of partial truths awaiting synthesis, not a congeries of errors demanding refutation" (Marshall Brown, "The Logic of Realism: A Hegelian Approach," *PMLA* 96 [1981]: 224).

'reality,' 'objectivity.' "[69] Although American realists themselves defended their movement with these labels, the terms
are not truly distinguishing. Most of them apply to good fiction of all traditions.

In attempting to make the explication of realism more concrete and verifiable, critics have turned increasingly to the issues of style and presentation. In many instances, however,
this shift from content to form is only window dressing. As
Kolb notes: "For many critics, the mere statement that style
is an important part of realism is enough, and they fail to discuss what that style is and how it operates."[70] Perhaps more
misleading is the critic who reduces realistic style to a conve-
nient formula—for example, the often-quoted Jakobsonian
observation that "it is the predominance of metonymy which
underlies and actually predetermines the so-called 'realistic'
trend"[71]—and uses it for interpretation. The style of realism
is as complex an issue as realism itself, for style is a reflection
of authorial intent and a measure of authorial effect, as well
as an integral element in the text. Moreover, as Jakobson himself has noted, what we think of as a realistic style can be either
radical or conservative. One artist might *"deform given artistic
norms . . . as an approximation of reality"* where another artist
might *"remain within the limits of a given artistic tradition . . . as
faithfulness to reality."*[72]

I do not propose in this study to offer a new definition of
realism nor to explicate all the variations that might fall under
the heading of realistic style. What I do want to argue is that
the three writers considered in this study represent the realistic tradition in American fiction, and their conception of real-

---

69. Kolb, *Illusion of Life*, p. 26.

70. Ibid., p. 57.

71. Roman Jakobson, "Two Aspects of Language and Two Types of Aphasic Disturbances," in *Fundamentals of Language*, ed. Jakobson and Morris Halle (The Hague:
Mouton & Co., 1956), p. 78.

72. Roman Jakobson, "On Realism in Art," in *Readings in Russian Poetics: Formalist
and Structuralist Views*, ed. Ladislav Matejka and Krystyna Pomorska (Ann Arbor:
Michigan Slavic Publications, 1978), p. 41.

ism rested as much on the presentation as on the content of their stories. Twain offers a lively summary of their position: "Style may be likened to an army, the author to its general, the book to the campaign."[73]

Some recent studies of the concept of literary realism have put the "army" back into the "campaign" in ways highly relevant to this inquiry. Terrence Doody, in tracing realism from *Don Quixote* to Joyce's *Ulysses*, develops a definition around the author's concept of the novel:

> These propositions are that the novel is a thing—not the author's self-expression so much as it is an object in its own right; that this kind of objective artifact entails the notion of an impersonal artist; and, most important, that the novelist who wants to create a thing and remain impersonal will necessarily be willing to undermine, distribute, or share his own authority in order to define his meaning by the proposal of a consensus rather than by an appeal to some superior or antecedent norm.[74]

The author who subscribes to these tenets confronts one of the paradoxes of realism: impersonality, or objectivity as writers like Howells label it, can be achieved only through a commitment to subjectivity. What results is the "anti-authoritarian nature of realism"[75] that depends for its expression on the recognition that "reality" varies from one person to the next and that even the individual point of view can and will change. As James put it in the "Preface to '*The Portrait of a Lady*'":

> Here we get exactly the high price of the novel as a literary form—its power not only, while preserving that form with closeness, to range through all the differences of the indi-

---

73. Samuel Langhorne Clemens, "Cooper's Prose Style," in *Letters from the Earth,* ed. Bernard DeVoto (New York: Harper & Row, 1962), p. 119.

74. Terrence Doody, "*Don Quixote, Ulysses,* and the Idea of Realism," *Novel* 12 (1979): 200.

75. Ibid., p. 214.

vidual relation to its general subject-matter, all the varieties of outlook on life, of disposition to reflect and project, created by conditions that are never the same from man to man (or, so far as that goes, from man to woman), but positively to appear more true to its character in proportion as it strains, or tends to burst, with a latent extravagance, its mould.[76]

Doody acknowledges that this concept of the novel derives from a particular world view: "Under this idea, things are meaningful in themselves; they do not refer for their significance to some higher or ulterior principle; they are, rather, immediately accessible to man's intelligence and amenable to the meaning he discovers and creates."[77] Doody may here be caught in what Marshall Brown calls "a mimetic or objective circle,"[78] but he grounds his explication of realism in several technical features, the most important of which involves the fact that realism creates "the necessity of omniscient authors who make no final claims for their omniscience, who in fact try to disguise or deny it by dealing it away."[79] Brown summarizes a similar explanation by Francis Hart: ". . . the narrative freedom of nineteenth-century novels was designed not to demonstrate the narrator's or author's omniscience but to test the possibilities and limits of omniscience."[80] William Stone offers yet another variation on this theme: "For a work to be termed an example of literary realism it must be able to impose an aesthetic order on its material, but it must do so *unobtrusively.*"[81] Ultimately, the technique should involve the reader as fully as possible in the unfolding of the story: "This then, is what we ask of literary realism, that it 'distance'

76. Henry James, *The Art of the Novel: Critical Prefaces*, intro. by Richard P. Blackmur (New York: Charles Scribner's Sons, 1962), pp. 45–6.
77. Doody, *"Don Quixote, Ulysses,* Idea of Realism," p. 201.
78. Brown, "The Logic of Realism," p. 225.
79. Doody, *"Don Quixote, Ulysses,* Idea of Realism," p. 213.
80. Brown, "The Logic of Realism," p. 228.
81. William Stone, "Towards a Definition of Literary Realism," *Centrum* 1 (Spring, 1973): 48.

us from the work of art only as far as is necessary for us to know it is a work of art."[82]

These critics clearly find a more persuasive explanation of realism in perspective than in the details of subject matter, but they do not overlook the intersection of the two. For example, Stone points out that one of the consequences of the technique he discusses is that character is favored over plot.[83] Kolb approaches a definition of American realism by tying antiomniscient narration to the authors' philosophy, morality, and subject matter. His explanation places American realists squarely within the tradition of European realism as exemplified by writers such as Flaubert, Daudet, Dostoyevsky, and Tolstoy.

Kolb sees point of view as "perhaps the most significant aspect of realistic style."[84] Basically, he equates point of view with the classical division between showing and telling or the slightly more complex division into "scene, picture, evaluation."[85] His summary of antiomniscience provides a good point of departure for this study: ". . . the realists' antiomniscience results in a twofold attempt to remove the external presence of the author through dramatic representation and through the effort to present description and summary, even when it is written in the third person (traditionally the territory of the omniscient author), from the angle of vision of the characters."[86]

In differing ways, James, Howells, and Twain sought to limit authorial involvement in the story. Twain was particularly successful with the "naïve" narrator—the simple, honest raconteur whose language is as limited as his experience. James found the innocent first-person narrator too restrictive, yet he strove to limit narrative perspective to a single con-

82. Ibid., p. 59.
83. Ibid., p. 56.
84. Kolb, *Illusion of Life*, p. 61.
85. Ibid., p. 66.
86. Ibid., p. 67.

sciousness. Of the three writers, Howells was the least concerned with techniques of narration, but he was the most concerned with "realistic" representation. He defined the author's moral responsibility to stick closely to the specifics of scene and dialogue and to remain "objective." As a result, his work is often antiomniscient by virtue of being "dramatic"; Howells preferred to show and let the reader see.

I have followed Kolb's example of limiting this study to works produced by James, Howells, and Twain in the 1884–86 period, although he discusses more works by each author. This period was a seminal one in the American realistic tradition, largely because of the work of these three novelists. All three novels included in this study treat the American scene, and all three have, to varying degrees, first-person narrators. They have in common narrative devices that are deliberately antiomniscient. *Adventures of Huckleberry Finn* and *The Rise of Silas Lapham* are generally considered to be masterpieces of their respective authors. *The Bostonians,* until recently, did not receive much critical attention; James did not revise it for the New York edition. I would argue, however, that it is not atypical of James's narrative technique. Although there is slightly more narrator intrusion than we find in some of his works, critics have discovered this pattern elsewhere,[87] and it is precisely the narrator's voice mingled with the presentation of several characters' speeches and thoughts that is of interest for this study. Although James's work in general has been much analyzed for its narrative technique, very little critical attention has been given to Howells' and Twain's manipulation of narrative modes. The study of narration and discourse in these three novels crucially affects their interpretation as well as providing evidence for the technical skill and innovativeness of each author.

---

87. John E. Tilford, Jr., "James the Old Intruder," *Modern Fiction Studies* 4 (1958): 157–60. See also W. R. Macnaughton, "The First-Person Narrators of Henry James," *Studies in American Fiction* 2 (1964): 145–64.

Useful as the concept of antiomniscience is, it is a general-ization in need of substantiation. If realism involves limita-tions on the author/narrator's role and representation of characters' perspectives, then a clearer understanding of point of view in fiction, based on the way in which character and narrator voices interact, is necessary to the exposition of the realistic style. I have shown in the earlier sections of this chapter how this understanding might be reached through the analysis of the language of the text. Such analysis should answer some of the questions that the discussion of realism raises. For example, how does an author/narrator demon-strate his antiomniscience? How does an author represent a character's perspective? How does an author arrive at a "com-mon vision," as Edwin Cady calls it,[88] through the representa-tion of individual perspectives? What I will demonstrate by analyses of narration and discourse in the three novels under consideration is the degree to which the American realists succeeded in the backgrounding of the author/narrator and the foregrounding of nonauthoritative/nonomniscient voices. Theirs were technical successes and failures that have profound significance for the development of the American novel's structure and for the portrayal of perception and the handling of point of view in later fiction.

James, Howells, and Twain differed somewhat in their tech-niques and subject matter, but they were united in their oppo-sition to the romance and the romantic tradition. Twain's attacks on Cooper and his charges against Sir Walter Scott, James's critique of Hawthorne, and Howells' general enthusi-asm for " 'banging the Babes of romance about' "[89] are all evidence of their line of attack. Yet these writers inherited from their predecessors a faith in the transforming power of language to capture reality. Implicit in the realists' faith in

88. Edwin Cady, *The Light of Common Day: Realism in American Fiction* (Bloomington and London: Indiana University Press, 1971), chapter 1 "Realism: Towards a Defini-tion," pp. 3–22.
89. Ibid., p. 7.

language to articulate a common vision and demonstrate the commonality of man are Emerson's views on literary language. Thus Emerson believed that ". . . wise men pierce this rotten diction and fasten words again to visible things. . . ."[90] This power to revitalize language results from recognizing the source of language in life: "Life is our dictionary. Years spent in country labors; in town; in the insight into trades and manufactures; in frank intercourse with many men and women; in science; in art; to the one end of mastering in all their facts a language by which to illustrate and embody our perceptions."[91] As the American spokesman for this doctrine, Emerson echoes Wordsworth and other romantics.

It is, therefore, not surprising that Perry Miller sees Twain's *Huckleberry Finn* as coming out of the same stylistic tradition as *Walden* and *Moby-Dick.* In *Huck Finn,* Twain adheres to "the Puritan determination to speak plainly, using art to conceal art, and metaphor suited to the common understanding."[92] This "plain style" was one of the tools the realists used to minimize the distance between reader and fiction, to make the author/narrator less obtrusive, and to create objectivity through subjectivity. If the realists inherited a philosophy of language and style, how did their practice actually differ from that of their predecessors? A brief look at the narrator's voice in *Moby-Dick* helps to establish the contrast.

Despite the parallelisms of its central sentence and the classical allusion, the opening paragraph of *Moby-Dick* establishes Ishmael as a straightforward, non-distanced narrator.

> Call me Ishmael. Some years ago—never mind how long precisely—having little or no money in my purse, and nothing particular to interest me on shore, I thought I

90. Ralph Waldo Emerson, "Nature," in *The Selected Writings of Ralph Waldo Emerson,* ed. Brooks Atkinson (New York: Random House, 1950), p. 17.
91. Emerson, "The American Scholar," in *Selected Writings,* p. 54.
92. Perry Miller, *Nature's Nation* (Cambridge: Belknap Press of Harvard University Press, 1967), p. 226.

would sail about a little and see the watery part of the world. It is a way I have of driving off the spleen, and regulating the circulation. Whenever I find myself growing grim about the mouth; whenever it is a damp, drizzly November in my soul; whenever I find myself involuntarily pausing before coffin warehouses, and bringing up the rear of every funeral I meet; and especially whenever my hypos get such an upper hand of me, that it requires a strong moral principle to prevent me from deliberately stepping into the street, and methodically knocking people's hats off—then, I account it high time to get to sea as soon as I can. This is my substitute for pistol and ball. With a philosophical flourish Cato throws himself upon his sword; I quietly take to the ship. There is nothing surprising in this. If they but knew it, almost all men in their degree, some time or other, cherish very nearly the same feelings toward the ocean with me.[93]

The narrative mode falls into Doležel's personal *Ich* category—"the direct discourse of a character carrying out representational function."[94] Though he is older than Huck Finn, Ishmael conveys some of Huck's self-effacing good humor. We are further reminded of Huck by Ishmael's use of qualifications, by the occasionally colloquial vocabulary, and by the unhurried pace of the paragraph. Huck, however, rarely succumbs to Ishmael's tendency toward generalization and inclusiveness, as demonstrated in the last sentence of the paragraph. In fact, many of Ishmael's passages beginning with personal experience end in more universal considerations.

The opening paragraph sets the tone for the novel's first section. The young Ishmael, mildly philosophic and moody, yet familiarly casual, narrates his tale. In the central section

93. Herman Melville, *Moby-Dick*, ed. Harrison Hayford and Hershel Parker (New York: W. W. Norton & Company, Inc., 1967), p. 12.
94. Doležel, *Narrative Modes*, p. 9.

of the novel, as Ishmael becomes more involved in the action, his narrative mode becomes more complex, reflecting his more sophisticated perception and his more demanding role as interpreter of events. Thus while tied to Queequeg, who is precariously balancing on a dead whale's back, Ishmael simultaneously relates and comments on his experience:

> So strongly and metaphysically did I conceive of my situation then, that while earnestly watching his motions, I seemed distinctly to perceive that my own individuality was now merged in a joint stock company of two: that my free will had received a mortal wound; and that another's mistake or misfortune might plunge innocent me into unmerited disaster and death. Therefore, I saw that here was a sort of interregnum in Providence; for its even-handed equity never could have sanctioned so gross an injustice. And yet still further pondering—while I jerked him now and then from between the whale and the ship, which would threaten to jam him—still further pondering, I say, I saw that this situation of mine was the precise situation of every mortal that breathes; only, in most cases, he, one way or other, has this Siamese connexion with a plurality of other mortals. . . .[95]

The narrator's voice is still a personal I, but it is now more insistently rhetorical and while he is more involved as a character, he is also more distanced as a narrator. His ironic philosophic speculations, which he offers without the slightest hesitation, demonstrate a striking detachment from the plight of Ishmael, the character.

As Ishmael's consciousness expands, his prominence both as character and as narrator diminishes. In fact, in the final dramatic sequence of the novel, the first-person narrator disappears. In his place we encounter an observing, occasionally rhetorical, third-person form. Here is his account of

95. Melville, *Moby-Dick*, p. 271.

some of the action of the final day of the chase after Moby Dick:

> At length as the craft was cast to one side, and ran ranging along with the White Whale's flank, he seemed strangely oblivious of its advance—as the whale sometimes will— and Ahab was fairly within the smoky mountain mist, which, thrown off from the whale's spout, curled round his great, Monadnock hump; he was even thus close to him; when, with body arched back, and both arms length-wise high-lifted to the poise, he darted his fierce iron, and his far fiercer curse into the hated whale. As both steel and curse sank to the socket, as if sucked into a morass, Moby Dick sideways writhed; spasmodically rolled his nigh flank against the bow, and, without staving a hole in it, so suddenly canted the boat over, that had it not been for the elevated part of the gunwale to which he then clung, Ahab would once more have been tossed into the sea. As it was, three of the oarsmen—who foreknew not the precise instant of the dart, and were therefore unprepared for its effects—these were flung out; but so fell, that, in an instant two of them clutched the gunwale again, and rising to its level on a combing wave, hurled themselves bodily inboard again; the third man helplessly dropping astern, but still afloat and swimming.[96]

The third man who is dropped astern, we later learn in the Epilogue, is Ishmael. Thus, while in the midst of the battle, he gives us only the action, foregoing any comment on his own reaction. And the narrator presents the action not from the perspective of the three oarsmen—"who foreknew not the precise instant of the dart"—but from the panoramic, retrospective view of an omniscient narrator.

Ishmael's involvement in his story ultimately enables him to transcend it. His retrospective account records his growing detachment. Knowledge and experience lead to authority, not

96. Ibid., p. 466.

ambiguity. Moreover, the voices of characters other than Ishmael, distinctive as they are, do not influence the narrator's voice and perspective. That voice becomes simultaneously more detached and more authoritative, a pattern quite opposite from the one we shall find in realistic fiction. What we will see in the realistic novel are narrators increasingly involved with and affected by the characters and the action of their stories. This involvement results in a loss of authority and reveals itself in a mingling of voices—the narrator's and the characters'—and ultimately a representation of multiple perspectives.

2

the
bostonians:
unresolved
ambiguity

The Bostonians (1886) falls in mid-career for James. *Portrait of a Lady* (1881) marked the climax of his early novel efforts; his later major period, probably delayed somewhat by the poor critical and public reception of *The Bostonians* and *The Princess Cassamassima* (1886), began with *The Wings of the Dove* (1902). James did not revise *The Bostonians* for the New York edition; yet, although he faulted it for weaknesses from time to time, he had a generally good opinion of the novel. Shortly after completing its serialization, he called it "the best fiction I have written."[1] However, a letter from William James (1885) prompted him to follow this initial evaluation with self-criticism. He wrote to William of "the redundancy of the book in the way of descriptive psychology" and somewhat later concluded that "all the middle part is too diffuse and insistent—far too descriptive and explaining and expatiating. The whole thing is too long and dawdling."[2] Much later (1908)

---

1. Henry James to William James, Feb. 14, 1885. (*The Letters of Henry James*, selected and edited by Percy Lubbock [New York: Octagon Books, 1970, rpt. of 1948 ed.] I: 117). Oscar Cargill, *The Novels of Henry James* (New York: Hefner Publishing Company, 1971), summarizes James's correspondence on the novel, pp. 131–34.

2. F. O. Matthiessen, *The James Family* (New York: Alfred A. Knopf, 1947), pp. 327 and 329.

he labeled it "tolerably full and good" in a letter to Howells.[3] Perhaps his most interesting comment in light of the study of narrative technique came in 1915 in a letter to Edmund Gosse. After its initial publication, he wrote, "I felt about it myself then that it was probably rather a remarkable feat of objectivity. . . ."[4]

Critical studies of the novel have given it mixed evaluations, although current studies do not reflect the hostility and contempt of American reviews when it was first published. On the one hand, J. W. Beach finds that the technique of the novel taxes the reader's patience, and the content offers "no perplexities of psychology or situation to be resolved."[5] At the opposite extreme, F. R. Leavis calls it "rich, intelligent, and brilliant" and a "very remarkable piece of psychological analysis."[6] Such diverse reactions result from ambiguity in the novel's technique and subject matter. While its wit and satiric force are often acclaimed,[7] critical discussion has centered primarily on thematic and character development and the relationship of these elements to social and political issues of the period. Considerable controversy exists concerning James's sympathy for his major characters and for their positions. Determining the novel's focus seems for many critics to come down to deciding whose point of view James shares or, at least, approves of. James's narrative technique and methods of discourse presentation, ranging in the novel from traditional narrator commentary to complex free indirect discourse, create ambiguity and make it difficult to determine his sympathies.

3. James, *Letters* II, p. 100.

4. Ibid., p. 498.

5. Joseph Warren Beach, *The Method of Henry James* (New Haven: Yale University Press, 1918), pp. 222 and 226.

6. F. R. Leavis, *The Great Tradition* (London: Chatto & Windus, 1948), pp. 138 and 135.

7. For example, Henry Seidel Canby says of the novel ". . . it is certainly one of his wittiest, and contains satiric passages not excelled elsewhere" (Henry Seidel Canby, *Turn West, Turn East: Mark Twain and Henry James* [New York: Biblo and Tannen, 1965], p. 174).

James himself commented on his narration in *The Bosto-nians*. In an 1899 letter to Julia Ward he notes that "there are . . . many magnificent and imperative cases . . . of presenting a thing by 'going behind' as many forms of consciousness as you like . . . I 'go behind' right and left in 'The Princess Cassa-massima,' 'The Bostonians,' 'The Tragic Muse'. . . ."[8] Thus in *The Bostonians* there is no rigid adherence to a single charac-ter's perspective nor does James limit intrusive narrator com-mentary as he does in his later work. In "The Art of Fiction" (1884),[9] which he completed shortly before starting *The Bosto-nians*, he describes the presentation he was probably striving for—a presentation based on views about realistic technique that he shared with both Howells and Twain. He asserts that the purpose of any novel is "to represent life."[10] The novelist must assume the role of historian; he betrays this responsibil-ity when he undermines the reality of his presentation by con-ceding "to the reader that he and this trusting friend are only 'making believe.' "[11] The intrusions of *The Bostonians* narra-tor often reassure the reader of the narrator's role as his-torian—as an honest, but far from omniscient, reporter of facts.

James further asserts in this essay that ". . . the air of reality (solidity of specification) seems to me to be the supreme vir-tue of a novel. . . ."[12] Not surprisingly, then, *The Bostonians* has been frequently praised for the realistic details of charac-terization and locale; as Howells indicates, " '. . . you go to the bottom of the half-frozen Cambridge mud.' "[13] Finally, James argues against the rigid separation of methods of expo-sition: "I cannot imagine composition existing in a series of

8. James, *Letters* I, pp. 324–25.

9. Henry James, "The Art of Fiction," in *The Portable Henry James*, ed. with intro. by Morton Dauwen Zabel, rev. by Lyall H. P. Powers (New York: The Viking Press, 1968), pp. 387–414.

10. Ibid., p. 389.

11. Ibid., p. 390.

12. Ibid., p. 399.

13. Cargill, *The Novels of Henry James*, p. 142.

blocks, nor conceive, in any novel worth discussing at all, of a passage of description that is not in its intention narrative, a passage of dialogue that is not in its intention descriptive . . ."[14] James draws freely on all manner of exposition in *The Bostonians;* he relies heavily on direct and varieties of indirect discourse (with the narrator's voice woven in) to develop his characters and theme. There are frequently no clear-cut boundaries between narrator exposition and the reported discourse of characters; each contributes to the whole.

narrator's voice

The narrator's voice in the novel is an interesting combination of authority and tentativeness. Because it fades in and out and does not exhibit the control we have come to associate with the later James, it has confused critics. In this respect, it is fortunate that James did not revise the work for the New York edition, for he would probably have tightened it and edited out some of the very interesting combinations of first-person narrator comment, third-person "objective" description, and the free intermingling of the narrator's voice with the voices of his characters. The mode here most clearly follows Doležel's "rhetorical-*Ich*" form. The first-person narrator "has his own voice," as Habegger notes,[15] and uses that voice to comment on and evaluate characters and action and to address the reader (always referred to in the third person). In his addresses to readers, his verb tenses usually refer to the time of reading rather than the time of the novel's action, as do related deictic markers.[16] "Olive may have been right,

14. James, "The Art of Fiction," p. 400.
15. Alfred Habegger, "The Disunity of *The Bostonians,*" *Nineteenth-Century Fiction* 24 (1969): 198.
16. Doležel describes *deixis* as "some demonstrative means [pronoun, adverbs] assume the function of pointing to the shifting time-space position of the speaking character . . ." (Lubomir Doležel, *Narrative Modes in Czech Literature* [Toronto and Buf-

but it shall be confided to the reader that in reality she never knew . . . whether Verena were a flirt or not."[17]

There are, however, large sections of third-person narrative exposition, sometimes "personalized through the employment of a character's tone of speech or thought," as Kolb notes,[18] where the first-person reference of the narrator disappears. Descriptive details in this novel are so freely offered and often demonstrate such wide-ranging knowledge of characters and scenes that one is tempted to call this narrator "omniscient," as Habegger does.[19] He is not bound by the immediately observable in a given scene nor by the information presented within the confines of the novel. James seems to favor "solidity of specification"—realism of detail rather than technique. The narrator freely judges his characters and their situations although he very scrupulously avoids judging the most crucial issues in the novel. Yet, James is not comfortable with his narrator's powers; he softens and downplays them. Thus, we are beset by qualifications: "I hardly know what illumination it was that sprang from her consciousness . . ."; "I know not exactly how these queer heresies had planted themselves . . ."; "I know not whether Basil was touched . . ."; "here, again I must plead a certain incompetence to give an answer."[20]

These notes of hesitation are absent from the first two-thirds of Book First; they are considerably more prominent in Book Second. In Book Third they are coupled with a certain reticence, "I scarcely venture to think now, what she [Olive] may have said to herself. . . ."[21] If we exclude impersonal narrative exposition, the amount of narrator "intru-

falo: University of Toronto Press, 1973], p. 28).

17. Henry James, *The Bostonians*, ed. with intro. by Irving Howe (New York: The Modern Library, Random House, 1956), p. 122.

18. Harold H. Kolb, Jr., *The Illusion of Life: American Realism as a Literary Form* (Charlottesville: The University Press of Virginia, 1969), p. 83.

19. Habegger, "The Disunity of *The Bostonians*," p. 198.

20. James, *The Bostonians*, pp. 164, 194, 283, and 423.

21. Ibid., p. 392.

sion" marked by either first-person pronominal references or "subjective semantics"[22] is far greater in Book First than in the subsequent books. This pattern confirms the observations of many critics that the novel's wit and satire (certainly facilitated by narrator commentary) are most prominent in the first book.

Habegger contrasts the narrator of Book First with that of Book Second as follows: "Book First is the fullest expression of one side of James—the Balzatian realist who surfaced throughout his life and flourished from 1878 to 1888 . . . Book Second is a less successful example of the second and major side of James—the psychological realist. . . ."[23] Book First's "all-judging, wide-ranging satiric persona," as Habegger calls him,[24] freely comments on his characters: "Poor Basil announced this fact to himself as if he had made a great discovery; but in reality he had never been so 'Boeotian' as at that moment"; "Her manner of repairing her inconsistency was altogether feminine . . ."; "Adeline's 'affairs,' as I have intimated, her social relations . . . her theory (for she had plenty of that, heaven save the mark!) . . . these things had been a subject of tragic consideration to Olive. . . ."[25] Moreover, this narrator takes charge of the reader: ". . . the reader, to whom, in the course of our history, I shall be under the necessity of imparting much occult information . . ."; "These considerations were not present to him as definitely as I have written them here . . ."; "These may be summed up in the remark . . . that two imperial women are scarcely more likely to hit it off together, as the phrase is, than two imperial men"; "I may as well say at once that she traversed most of this period without further serious alarms."[26] These last comments indicate the narrator's willingness to condense with summary—a

22. See chapter 1, fn. 61.
23. Habegger, "The Disunity of *The Bostonians*," p. 209.
24. Ibid., p. 205.
25. James, *The Bostonians*, pp. 11, 141, and 162.
26. Ibid., pp. 10, 11, 165, and 175.

pattern James avoided in later works. It is the most straightforward, least subtle way to deal with the "explosive principle," as James called it,[27] the tendency of material to expand
endlessly. In the narrator's most obvious use of summary in
The Bostonians (as in the examples above), he interjects a note
of (rhetorical-*Ich*) commentary, thus minimizing the air of
"make-believe" by offering the information as "personal" tes-
timony.

The narrator also uses less obvious forms of summary,
often involving a character's thought-process or a mixture of
thought and narrator comment. Habegger comments on one
interesting passage of this type which captures the ironic tone
of Book First: "Olive Chancellor offered Basil Ransom a
greeting which she believed to be consummately ladylike, and
which the young man, narrating the scene several months
later to Mrs. Luna, whose susceptibilities he did not feel
obliged to consider (she considered his so little), described
by saying that she glared at him."[28] The language here is primarily the narrator's, although the parenthetical— "(she considered his so little)"—and the indirectly reported speech—
"she glared at him"—may be Ransom's responsibility. The
narrator allows himself inside views of both Ransom and
Olive—a bit of "omniscience." He also freely mingles perspectives, beginning with Olive and switching to Basil, and
time periods. Habegger finds that such "foreshortening"
and its ironic effects are largely missing from Book Second
where the narrator is restricted by the necessity of "main-
taining a consistent point of view" and "a strict and confin-
ing chronology."[29] I would agree with Habegger that the
narrator relies more on the characters' points of view
in Book Second, but this control is far from consistent.

27. Henry L. Terrie, Jr. cites James's use of this phrase from *The Novels and Tales
of Henry James* XVIII: xv, in his essay "Henry James and the 'Explosive Principle,' "
Nineteenth-Century Fiction 15 (1961): 283.
28. James, *The Bostonians*, p. 88.
29. Habegger, "The Disunity of *The Bostonians*," p. 203.

The second book opens with a leisurely description of Basil's New York setting and his frame of mind several months after his first visit to Boston. The description of his setting is, as David Howard notes, "frankly personal and also apparently frankly irrelevant."[30] Thus, the narrator, continuing his personal intervention, says, "I mention it [a Dutch grocery] not on account of any particular influence it may have had on the life or the thought of Basil Ransom, but for old acquaintance sake and that of local color. . . ."[31] The narrator continues with some ambivalence, defending his description, "a figure is nothing without a setting," but suggesting, rather coyly, his narrative discretion, "if the opportunity were not denied me here, I should like to give some accounts of Basil Ransom's interior."[32]

Comments on narrative technique are prominent in this book suggesting "a strangely fussy uneasiness."[33] They often combine with addresses to or comments about the reader and with a tone of increasing tentativeness that is probably meant to undermine the narrator's apparent "omniscience." Thus, in describing Basil's position, the narrator starts on a positive note, "I shall not attempt a complete description of Ransom's ill-starred views, being convinced that the reader will guess them as he goes, for they had a frolicsome, ingenious way of peeping out of the young man's conversation."[34] A few pages later he takes the same forceful and somewhat conspiratorial tone when he says, "when I have added that he hated to see women eager and argumentative, . . . I shall have sketched a state of mind which will doubtless strike many readers as painfully crude."[35] Such authoritative statements mingle in Book Second with a much more tentative narration that even-

30. David Howard, *"The Bostonians,"* pp. 60–80 in *The Air of Reality: New Essays on Henry James*, ed. John Goode (London: Metheun & Co. Ltd., 1972), p. 64.
31. James, *The Bostonians*, p. 190.
32. Ibid., p. 191.
33. Habegger, "The Disunity of *The Bostonians*," p. 204.
34. James, *The Bostonians*, p. 194.
35. Ibid., p. 198.

tually comes to dominate. On the one hand, the narrator appears to base his conclusions about Basil on Basil's own utterances—"I suppose he was very conceited, for he was much addicted to judging his age."[36] Yet only a few sentences later he authoritatively offers the reader information that Basil has never divulged—"He liked his pedigree, he revered his forefathers and he rather pitied those who might come after him. In saying so, however, I betray him a little, for he never mentioned such feelings as these."[37]

The same ambivalence surfaces somewhat later in the Book when the narrator comments on the first private encounter between Verena and Basil. In introductions to Verena's direct discourse, the narrator speculates about conclusions the reader might draw from the discourse itself: "I know not whether Verena was provoked, but she answered with more spirit than sequence . . ."; "It is very possible that Verena was provoked, inaccessible as she was, in a general way, to irritation; for she rejoined in a moment. . . ."[38] Yet, rather abruptly, the narrator drops this objective stance to explore Verena's thoughts: "It may be communicated to the reader that it was very agreeable to Verena to learn that her visitor had made this arduous pilgrimage . . . with only half the prospect of reward. . . ."[39]

In Book Second the narrator continues to offer opinions on his characters. He contrasts Olive and Adeline: "In reality, Olive was distinguished and discriminating, and Adeline was the dupe . . ."; of Basil he says "the poor fellow delivered himself of these narrow notions (the rejection of which by leading periodicals was certainly not a matter of surprise). . . ."[40] At the same time, the narrator feels the awkwardness of his presence, referring to himself as the "chronicler" or "the historian who gathered these documents" and involving the reader

36. Ibid., p. 194.
37. Ibid., p. 195.
38. Ibid., p. 235.
39. Ibid.
40. Ibid., pp. 199 and 343.

rather clumsily in his narration: "I shall perhaps expose our young man to the contempt of superior minds if I say . . ."; "If we were at this moment to take, in a single glance, an inside view of Mrs. Burrage (a liberty we have not yet ventured on), I suspect . . ."; "If the moment I speak of had lasted a few seconds longer I know not what monstrous proceeding of this kind it would have been my difficult duty to describe. . . ."[41] On the whole, the narrator's voice in Book Second exercises less control than in Book First, but it is more obtrusive. More space is given over to characters' speech and thought, most often rendered indirectly, and although this material requires a narrator's presence, it foregrounds the characters' voices and pushes the narrator into a less prominent role.

The notes of qualification and uncertainty introduced in Book Second are struck with increasing frequency in Book Third. The narrator reflects in his own professions of inadequacy the profound emotional experiences of each of his characters. "No stranger situation can be imagined than that of these extraordinary young women at this juncture . . . I despair of presenting it to the reader with the air of reality."[42]

This skepticism makes "the air of reality" all the more insistent; the narrator's reticence makes him an observer like the reader: "But I scarcely venture to think now what she [Olive] may have said to herself . . . From Olive's conditions . . . there is a certain propriety . . . in averting our head"; "These are mysteries into which I shall not attempt to enter, speculations with which I have no concern . . ."; "Here again I must plead a certain incompetence to give an answer . . ."; "I know not whether Ransom would have attempted to answer her question had an obstacle not presented itself. . . ."[43]

Although the narrator allows himself an occasional

41. Ibid., pp. 341, 274, 328, 319, and 340.
42. Ibid., p. 391. Note the echo from "The Art of Fiction": ". . . the air of reality . . . seems to me to be the supreme virtue of a novel . . ." (cited on p. 39 above).
43. Ibid., pp. 392, 422, 423, and 435.

straightforward judgment ("Olive thought she knew the worst, as we have perceived; but the worst was really something she could not know . . .")[44] and freely uses adjectives (e.g., *poor*) to label the predicaments of his characters, he restricts himself much more rigidly in this book to the views of the characters themselves as expressed in their thought and speech. This pattern, begun in earnest in Book Second, contributes to the novel's suspense because we see the potential outcome primarily through the characters' eyes. To use Franz Stanzel's typology, we shift from the largely external narrative experience of Book First to the internal, limited perspective of the characters themselves in Book Third.[45] We have throughout a first-person narrator who is quite separate from any of his characters, so that the transition from external to internal must be accomplished by a greater use of reported discourse of all kinds that allows the characters to become reflectors.

directly reported discourse

Of the three novels examined in this study, only *The Bostonians* opens with directly reported discourse (DD). Our initial impressions of the characters result primarily from their own speech in dramatic interchanges with one another. In fact, the use of language is part of the novel's theme. All three central characters are good "talkers." Verena's public recognition and initial appeal for Olive is her ability to "speechify." The act of speaking is more important to Verena than the substance behind the speech. Olive asserts her claims on Verena by the passion with which she engages her in conversation, but Basil finally wins Verena over, at

44. Ibid., p. 395.
45. Franz K. Stanzel, "Second Thoughts on *Narrative Situations in the Novel: Towards a 'Grammar of Fiction,'* " *Novel* 11 (1979): 257.

least in part, with his rhetoric. The three characters introduced in chapter 1 (Olive, Basil, and Mrs. Luna) are described in terms of the actual quality of their speech. Mrs.
Luna's opening remarks are "spoken with much voluabili-
ty"; Olive's voice "was low and agreeable—a cultivated
voice."[46] The narrator takes the greatest pains in describing
Basil's speech:

> And yet the reader who likes a complete image, who de-
> sires to read with the senses as well as with the reason,
> is entreated not to forget that he [Basil] prolonged his
> consonants and swallowed his vowels, that he was guilty
> of elisions and interpolations which were equally unex-
> pected, and that his discourse was pervaded by something
> sultry and vast, something almost African in its rich, bask-
> ing tone, something that suggested the teeming expanse
> of the cotton field.[47]

Comments such as these indicate James's sensitivity to the
speaking voice and to the reflections of character it may contain.[48] For example, Ransom seems to hide behind his accent,
invoking it most heavily when he is least sincere. Thus, in an
exchange with Mrs. Luna, the narrator tells us that Ransom's
compliment involves "the tone Mrs. Luna always found so unsatisfactory. It was a part of his Southern gallantry—his accent
always came out strongly when he said anything of that sort—
and it committed him to nothing in particular."[49] A comment
of Basil's to Miss Birdseye is sincere because he downplays
his accent: "Ransom found himself liking Miss Birdseye very
much, and it was quite without hypocrisy or a tinge too much
of the local quality in his speech that he said: 'Wherever you

46. James, *The Bostonians*, pp. 3 and 8.
47. Ibid., p. 5.
48. The narrator makes only minimal use of "eye-dialect" (spelling meant to reflect a character's peculiar pronunciation), limiting it to the speech of "humorous"
characters like the Tarrants.
49. James, *The Bostonians*, p. 203.

go, madam, it will matter little what you carry. You will always carry your goodness."[50]

In addition to describing the idiosyncratic features of his characters' speech, the narrator comments on the characters' reactions to one another's speech in "stage directions," as Twain called the tags introducing or following directly reported discourse.[51] Many critics have cited the importance of "talk," dialogue, in carrying forward James's novels and short stories, but almost as important as the talk itself are the ways in which characters "take it in," "turn it over," and "see" as a consequence of listening. James's narrators run the gamut of discourse commentary from a Hemingway-like bareness— dialogues with no comment—to a series of sentences, much more copious than ordinary tags, alternating with the direct discourse itself—enriching and expanding the reader's experience of speech. Tags on direct discourse are also one of the simplest ways for the narrator to comment on the characters and action. When he describes a character's tone or attitude in speaking, he places himself on the scene and offers his opinions on the characters.

More interesting perhaps is the way in which this narrator uses tags to indicate that his observations are speculative, not omniscient. Two qualifiers, *apparently* and *evidently,* which appear frequently in the novel, are conspicuous in the tags: ". . . then he said in a tone which evidently was carefully considerate . . ."; "This speech on Verena's part was evidently perfunctory . . ."; "She listened with great reserve, and apparently thought it over a little—she was evidently addicted neither to empty phrases nor to unconsidered assertions"; ". . . said Ransom, with a sadness which Mrs. Luna evidently regarded as a refinement of outrage."[52]

50. Ibid., p. 220.

51. Samuel L. Clemens, "William Dean Howells," rpt. in *Howells: A Century of Criticism,* ed. Kenneth E. Eble (Dallas: Southern Methodist University Press, 1962), p. 85.

52. James, *The Bostonians,* pp. 220, 251, 360, and 430.

Dialogues provide the drama in *The Bostonians* and reveal a great deal about the characters involved. All the characters, minor and major, are given an opportunity to reveal themselves in their own words. With minor characters, direct discourse often takes the form of long monologues. The characters seem to talk for the sake of hearing themselves talk. Moreover, the narrator uses the speech of characters like the Tarrants and Matthias Pardon to satirize them. For example, in Book First Mrs. Tarrant addresses Olive with a rambling, repetitive monologue guaranteed to annoy Olive with its triviality.

> ". . . Mr. Gracie is very different; he is intensely plain, but I believe he is very learned. You don't think him plain? Oh, you don't know? Well, I suppose you don't care, you must see so many. But I must say, when a young man looks like that, I call him painfully plain. . . ."[53]

Not only does this sort of speech capture better than any description Mrs. Tarrant's inconsequentiality and empty-headedness, it also offers, as S. Gorley Putt notes, "a wincing appreciation of every last scrap of vulgarity in nineteenth-century American domestic conversation. . . ."[54]

Some minor characters figure in the novel as observers. The direct discourse of Mrs. Luna and Dr. Prance not only reveals their personalities, the former witty, sarcastic, fatuous, the latter wry and resigned, but also adds important information to the story. Thus, when Mrs. Luna comments on Verena to Basil, her conclusions foreshadow ironically the outcome of the story: " 'But, mark my words,' said Mrs. Luna, 'she will give Olive the greatest cut she has ever had in her life. She will run off with some lion-tamer; she will marry a circus-man!' "[55]

The form of dialogues, particularly between major charac-

53. Ibid., p. 121.

54. S. Gorley Putt, *Henry James: A Reader's Guide* (Ithaca, New York: Cornell University Press, 1966), p. 183.

55. James, *The Bostonians,* p. 210.

ters, marks a midway point in James's career. They are less stilted than those we find in earlier works and less elliptical (and therefore less portentous) than those in the later works. They often involve the repetition by two characters of a key word or phrase that has a slightly, or radically, different meaning for each. Usually each character retains his perspective, so the dialogues air views without the painstaking efforts at resolution that we find in the later works. Ruth Yeazell has noted that ". . . for so many late Jamesian characters, talking becomes a form of thinking aloud"; characters gain insight by "echoing . . . [and] expanding each other's language. . . ."[56] In the early novels, as exemplified by *The American*, characters "keep their verbal and imaginative distance"; "They do not build on one another's formulations. . . ."[57] *The Bostonians* falls somewhere between these extremes. Dialogues reveal characters to one another and to the reader without necessarily involving them in mutual interpretations of the same subject. They are often combative rather than conciliatory; dramatic clashes rather than dramatic revelations are the keynote.

One of Olive and Verena's first exchanges demonstrates Verena's simplicity, bordering on simplemindedness, contrasted with Olive's intensity. Repetition stresses concepts and suggests the different perspectives of the two characters.

> "There is so much I want to ask you," said Olive.
> "Well, I can't say much except when father has worked on me," Verena answered, with an ingenuousness beside which humility would have seemed pretentious.
> "I don't care anything about your father," Olive rejoined very gravely, with a great air of security.
> "He is very good," Verena said simply. "And he's wonderfully magnetic."

56. Ruth Bernard Yeazell, *Language and Knowledge in the Late Novels of Henry James* (Chicago and London: The University of Chicago Press, 1976), pp. 89 and 67.
57. Ibid., pp. 67 and 66.

"It isn't your father, and it isn't your mother; I don't
think of them, and it's not them I want. It's only you—just
as you are."

Verena dropped her eyes to the front of her dress. "Just
as she was" seemed to her indeed very well.

"Do you want me to give up—?" she demanded, smiling.

Olive Chancellor drew in her breath for an instant, like
a creature in pain; then, with her quavering voice,
touched with a vibration of anguish, she said: "Oh, how
can I ask you to give up? *I* will give up—I will give up
everything!"[58]

This dialogue neatly captures the personalities of the two
women. Olive's statements throughout the book are usually
"very grave" or very intense, "touched with a vibration of anguish." She has little skill or time for light discourse—an "attempted pleasantry on Miss Chancellor's part" is "so
unexpected, so incongruous, uttered with white lips and cold
eyes."[59]

Verena's simplicity emerges in several ways. She naively assumes that Olive is attracted to her because of her "gift"—an
assumption that forces Olive's desire to possess Verena
wholly to a more brutal expression. She is honest, not humble, about her "gift"—the narrator's comment implies that
she would have to know pride to know humility. She is, however, pleased with her appearance, which the reader knows
from other descriptions to be a bit fantastic. Olive wants
Verena's soul, but Olive's passionate avowal, starkly presented without a tag, prompts Verena to contemplate her
dress. The free indirect repetition of Olive's statement, "just
as she was," signals either the impact of the idea on Verena
or her actual repeating of it to herself. Although it occurs in
quotes, the past tense and third person make it free indirect,

58. James, *The Bostonians*, p. 58.
59. Ibid., p. 376.

and thus it leads very smoothly into her reaction, the "indeed very well" portion representing Verena's, not the narrator's, judgment.

The dialogue concludes with a typically Jamesian exchange on a key phrase, "give up," which is repeated throughout the novel along with the related "renounce." Here the dash after Verena's "give up" seems to leave open the question of what she is to give up—her work, her parents, her individuality? Interestingly enough, the narrator tells us at the beginning of the chapter in which we find this exchange that "from this first interview she [Verena] felt that she was seized, and she gave herself up, only shutting her eyes a little, as we do whenever a person in whom we have perfect confidence proposes, with our assent, to subject us to some sensation."[60] It would seem that Verena gives up any resistance to Olive, that is, puts herself wholly in Olive's hands. But in the dialogue itself, it is Olive who vows total renunciation and Verena, at that moment, seems to associate Olive's "giving up" with Olive's wealth and social position. The dialogue tells the reader more about the characters than they themselves know.

A dramatic exchange between Basil and Olive in Book Second reveals the depth of their mutual misunderstanding and the narrator's apparent sympathy at this juncture for Olive.

> Olive took no notice of his remark as to how she herself might be affected by his visit; but she asked in a moment why he should think it necessary to call on Miss Tarrant. "You know you are not in sympathy," she added, in a tone which contained a really touching element of entreaty that he would not even pretend to prove he was.
>
> I know not whether Basil was touched, but he said, with every appearance of a conciliatory purpose—"I wish to thank her for all the interesting information she has given me this evening."
>
> "If you think it generous to come and scoff at her, of

60. Ibid., p. 79.

course she has no defense; you will be glad to know that."

"Dear Miss Chancellor, if you are not a defense—a bat-
tery of many guns!" Ransom exclaimed.

"Well, she at least is not mine!" Olive returned, spring-
ing to her feet. She looked round her as if she were really
pressed too hard, panting like a hunted creature.

"Your defense is your certain immunity from attack.
Perhaps if you won't tell me where you are staying, you
will kindly ask Miss Tarrant herself to do so. Would she
send me a word on a card?"

"We are in West Tenth Street," Olive said; and she
gave the number. "Of course you are free to come."

"Of course I am! Why shouldn't I be? But I am greatly
obliged to you for the information. I will ask her to come
out, so that you won't see us." And he turned away, with
the sense that it was really insufferable, her attempt always to give him the air of being in the wrong.[61]

Basil has undertaken to ask Olive for her address in New
York rather than to get it from Mrs. Luna because "it is better
that this interference [between Olive and Verena] should be
accompanied by all the forms of chivalry."[62] This interpretation, presented from Basil's perspective, involves some self-
deception. He thinks he wants to be decent to Olive, but he
also wants his own way and at this point in the narrative, he
has so grievously insulted Mrs. Luna that there is every possibility she will turn him down. Moreover, while he is being
honest about his plans to visit, he is also challenging Olive
to refuse him. He clearly feels that he has the upper hand,
and he is confident of Verena's accessibility should Olive refuse him.

Olive's initial reaction to Basil's request is quite inhospita-
ble. The narrator softens it by presenting it as indirect discourse and by reporting directly her excuse for her rudeness.
The narrator's comment on her statement reflects some sym-

61. Ibid., pp. 282–83.
62. Ibid., p. 282.

pathy, especially the emphatic "really" which might indicate the depth to which the reader should be touched or which might be intended to overcome the reader's skepticism about Olive's ability to make a touching statement. Basil does, in fact, respond to her implied entreaty for him to demonstrate some sympathy, but the narrator leaves his actual reaction to Olive ambiguous by a plea of his own to ignorance. Moreover, the narrator gives no indication of Basil's tone. Basil's response "appears" to be conciliatory; it is certainly polite, but it is also a lie, and Olive seems to sense sarcasm in it.

Olive's rather self-righteous plea of defenselessness evokes from him a response both patronizing, "dear Miss Chancellor," and mocking, "a defense of guns." This attack is so threatening that the reader's sympathy is again invoked, although this time Olive is distanced as the narrator compares her to an animal. She does not know at this point the source of Basil's persistence or incivility. Although the narrator again presents Basil's response without comment on his tone, Basil would seem to be sarcastic rather than admiring in his reference to Olive's "immunity." She is either too formidable to be broached or, more likely, too unfeminine and ungracious to be worthy of approach. By contrasting her to Verena, he implies that Verena is better-humored and -mannered; moreover, he implies an intimacy with Verena that works like a threat against Olive. Olive capitulates when faced with his persistence; she clearly loses the confrontation. Basil's parting comment about asking Verena out strikes again at Olive's lack of hospitality and also suggests a control over Verena which threatens Olive. He leaves with outraged sensibilities, but the narrator's sympathies are not necessarily with him. He has not been particularly "decent."

Directly reported discourse offers the narrator ample opportunity to guide the reader's perceptions, but the comments of the narrator are rigidly separated from the actual words of the participants. A far more subtle way to introduce narrator comment into dialogue is to mingle direct reports with various indirectly reported forms.

indirectly reported discourse

The narrator of *The Bostonians* uses a range of indirectly reported speech and thought (ID) from summaries of speech that contain the character's sentiments but not necessarily his words to apparently verbatim accounts of speeches and thoughts with only the minimum changes necessary for indirection of the "free" or compact type—changes in pronominal forms and verb tenses. The reports themselves are introduced by a variety of tags, and several methods of reporting often mix together in the same account. Thus we might move from narrator's summary into a character's thoughts or words into a combination of the two, and back to summary, in the course of a few sentences.

These sentences maintain the rhythms we associate with speech rather than writing. Pauses, parenthetical asides, repetitions, idiosyncratic phrases associated with given characters' direct discourse (in short, direct discourse features integrated into the narrative base) evoke the colloquial quality of speech without rendering the discourse directly. James's tendency to permit the qualities abstracted from spoken language to spill over from directly reported speech to indirectly reported discourse may have extended even to the colloquialization of narration involving no discourse at all, as Richard Bridgman asserts.[63] Certainly, the indirect reports of speech are the models he used to present the characters' thoughts. Moreover, by varying his reports of discourse, the narrator achieves a "splendid *economy* to which his long sentences and inflated periphrasis so oddly and actively contribute. . . ."[64]

The effects of these indirect reports are as varied as their forms. They may, by virtue of what is apparently left out, suggest the economical rendering of a long-winded conversation,

---

63. Richard Bridgman, *The Colloquial Style in America* (New York: Oxford University Press, 1968), p. 98.
64. Putt, *Henry James*, p. 181.

or they may extend an apparently brief conversation or thought sequence with narrator commentary. Most important, however, is the way indirection as a technique of narration manipulates the reader's perceptions of characters and events within the novel. Indirect reports create both distance and ambiguity. In directly reported dialogues, the reader may be uncertain about the implications of what a character says, and in this sense is aided both by narrator comment and the reaction of the other participants in the conversation, but in indirectly reported discourse the reader must constantly ask whose linguistic responsibility the indirect report represents. For example, when the narrator tells us that ". . . she [Olive] was very eloquent when she reminded Verena how the exquisite weakness of women had never been their defense, but had only exposed them to sufferings more acute than masculine grossness can conceive,"[65] we must assume that the indirectly reported portion beginning "how the exquisite weakness of women" is the narrator's summary of many conversations, filled with specific examples, that Olive and Verena have had on the suffering of women. In fact, the summary itself is so "eloquent" that it is suspiciously ironic.

In other reports the narrator explicitly identifies words actually uttered by the character: ". . . he [Basil] contented himself with saying that he must condone his Boeotian ignorance (he was fond of an elegant phrase). . . ."[66] Not only does the narrator absolve himself from responsibility for the phrase with his parenthetical, later when he uses the adjective *Boeotian* to describe Basil (". . . in reality he had never been so 'Boeotian' as at that moment"),[67] he puts it in quotation marks. Another more complicated example of this assigning of responsibility involves a summary of a dialogue between Verena and Olive.

---

65. James, *The Bostonians*, p. 185.
66. Ibid., p. 7.
67. Ibid., p. 11.

> When Miss Chancellor asked if she [Verena] respected
> Mr. Burrage (and how solemn Olive could make that
> word she by this time knew), she answered with her sweet,
> vain laugh, but apparently with perfect good faith, that
> it didn't matter whether she did or not, for what was the
> whole thing but simply a phase—the very one they had
> talked about?[68]

At least two elements in this ID are the reported speakers'
responsibility. Judging from the narrator's parenthetical comment, one assumes that Olive actually uses the word *respect.*
Verena's indirectly reported statement beginning with the
question/exclamation "for what" is apparently a free indirect
rendering (compact ID) of her exact words. The question itself is not embeddable—"she answered that for what . . ."
—and the word *phase* refers to other conversations and therefore must have been used here. The narrator's comment on
this exchange, "she answered with her sweet, vain laugh, but
apparently with perfect good faith," resembles the tags of direct discourse. The *apparently* casts doubt both on the narrator's knowledge and on Verena's good faith. The narrator
must be held responsible for the adjectives *sweet, vain,* but
since Olive depends on Verena's good faith, the *apparently* may
be a reflection of her view rather than the narrator's qualifier.

Additional examples of ID in which the responsibility for
certain elements (expressive adjectives, stress, emotive function) belongs to the reported speaker abound. For example,
emphatic expressions usually limited to direct discourse and
signalling the emotive function occur frequently in ID.

> Verena said she *did* think she had a certain amount of
> imagination. . . .[69]
>
> . . . [Olive] declared that she didn't know why Mrs. Bur-
> rage addressed herself to *her,* that Miss Tarrant was free

68. Ibid., p. 151.
69. Ibid., p. 86.

as air, that her future was in her own hands, that such a
matter as this was a kind of thing with which it could never
occur to one to interfere.[70]

In a few cases with minor characters' speech, features identi-
fied as dialect appear in ID.

He [Mr. Tarrant] added, presently, that he supposed he
should have to fix it with Mis' Tarrant. . . .[71]

In a subtler way, the colloquialness of some embedded
phrases suggests that they are meant to represent the direct
discourse of the reported speaker. Thus, Mrs. Tarrant whose
indirectly reported speech (like her husband's) is highlighted
with dialect spellings—*prop'ty, fam'ly*[72] has the same tone in
directly and indirectly reported speech.

Mrs. Tarrant . . . said she didn't know as she was fit to
struggle alone, and that, half the time, if Verena was away,
she wouldn't have the nerve to answer the doorbell. . . .[73]

Unmarked direct discourse (direct discourse presented
with no quotation marks), the form used most often to convey
interior monologue, is the only type of report absent from *The
Bostonians*. All insights into characters' thoughts retain the indirection of at least the third-person pronouns and the past
tense. Except in directly reported speech, the *I*'s of the text
refer exclusively to the narrator.

minor characters' indirectly reported discourse

When the narrator combines a variety of methods to
report the speech of minor characters, the reader gets a sense
of these characters' speaking without actually having to listen
to them. This technique works most consistently in Book First

70. Ibid., p. 318.
71. Ibid., p. 169.
72. Ibid., pp. 120 and 121.
73. Ibid., p. 171.

and accounts for the satiric tone of that section. The idiosyncrasies of the characters' compact ID keeps the reader at a distance, and the frequency of narrator comments interspersed
in the reports makes the perspective external. For example,
a sentence above, if quoted fully, shows an interesting pro-
gression from narrator summary to ID, both diffused and
compact, to narrator comment.

> Mrs. Tarrant sighed and grimaced, wrapped herself more
> than ever in her mantle, said she didn't know as she was
> fit to struggle alone, and that, half the time, if Verena was
> away she wouldn't have the nerve to answer the doorbell;
> she was incapable, of course, of neglecting such an oppor-
> tunity to posture as one who paid with her heart's blood
> for leading the van of human progress.[74]

The narrator's final comment is very clearly mocking, but it
also represents the "inflated periphrasis" that Putt discusses.
Though Mrs. Tarrant is posing, the pose itself is described
as she would have seen it. As Putt notes, "sarcasm is altogether too simple a label for these apparent verbal absurdi-
ties; there is a very real sense in which each one of them is
true, more true than the simpler paraphrase, because in smiling at them we remember that from the *inside* of the mind of
the character concerned there is nothing funny in the tone."[75]
Yet, we are not inside but outside and the wit becomes double-edged, capturing and mocking her pretension to gentility.

In Book First the indirectly reported discourse of minor
characters often summarizes a scene or a series of events dramatically, keeping the tone of the participants in evidence. In
chapter 1, Mrs. Luna's rather fatuous conversation provides
the background for Olive and Basil's first meeting. Before
they can even exchange greetings, Mrs. Luna breaks in—first
indirectly and then directly.

74. Ibid.
75. Putt, *Henry James,* p. 193.

> Mrs. Luna explained to her sister that her freedom of speech was caused by his being a relation—though, indeed, he didn't seem to know much about them. She didn't believe he had ever heard of her, Mrs. Luna, though he pretended, with his Southern chivalry, that he had. She must be off to her dinner now, she saw the carriage was there, and in her absence Olive might give any version of her she chose.[76]

Beginning as indirectly reported discourse, a verb of saying *(explain)* followed by a subordinate clause that seems likely to be the narrator's summary (the gerund construction is unusual in direct discourse), the first sentence drifts into compact ID. After the dash, the exclamatory *indeed* and the contraction *didn't* add a colloquial, personal note that makes these Mrs. Luna's own words filtered through a narrator's report. Subsequent DD features include the emphatic, *Mrs. Luna,* a self-centered reference all the more ridiculous for its indirect presentation, the present deictic *now* coupled with the subjective *must,* and the run-on, breathless quality of the last sentence. This last sentence seems to move out of compact ID—away from an almost direct report of Mrs. Luna's words—with the deictic *there* instead of *here* and the summary implied in the last clause.

Mrs. Luna's ID suggests that she is long-winded and self-centered, but the narrator also uses rather lengthy indirect reports to compress the speeches of characters he portrays sympathetically. Dr. Prance is a woman of strong opinions, but she is not an eager conversationalist and it takes some strong stimulus (in this case, irritation) to get her to offer her thoughts. The narrator uses her to introduce other characters at Miss Birdseye's evening to Basil by giving her an indirectly reported monologue. The monologue evolves from the narration itself without any clear introduction and its form vacillates between diffused and compact. The narrator has given

76. Ibid., pp. 8–9.

some of Basil's impressions of Dr. Prance ("this little lady was tough and technical; she evidently didn't care for great movements . . ."),[77] and Basil and Dr. Prance have engaged in a directly reported exchange on the women's movement, followed by some reported discourse. Narrator summary intervenes:

> Ransom became so sensible of this that he felt it was indelicate to allude further to the cause of woman, and, for a change, endeavored to elicit from his companion some information about the gentlemen present. He had given her a chance, vainly, to start some topic herself; but he could see that she had no interests beyond the researches from which, this evening, she had been torn, and was incapable of asking him a personal question. She knew two or three of the gentlemen; she had seen them before at Miss Birdseye's. Of course she knew principally ladies. . . .[78]

The first sentence seems to be the summary of an omniscient narrator; the second makes specific reference to Basil's perspective ("he could see"). Sentence three might be narrator summary, but the "of course" of the following sentence makes it likely that three itself is the onset of Dr. Prance's indirectly reported speech that continues in monologue form. The descriptions of Matthias Pardon and Selah Tarrant that follow are clearly compact ID.

> She knew Mr. Pardon; that was the young man with the "side-whiskers" and the white hair; he was a kind of editor, and he wrote, too, "over his signature"—perhaps Basil had read some of his works; he was under thirty, in spite of his white hair. He was a great deal thought of in magazine circles. She believed he was very bright—but she hadn't read anything. She didn't read much—not for

77. Ibid., p. 43.
78. Ibid.

amusement; only the "Transcript." She believed Mr. Pardon sometimes wrote in the "Transcript"; well, she supposed he *was* very bright. The other that she knew—only she didn't know him (she supposed Basil would think that queer)—was the tall, pale gentleman, with the black mustache and the eye-glass. She knew him because she had met him in society; but, she didn't know him—well, because she didn't want to. If he should come and speak to her—and he looked as if he were going to work round that way—she should just say to him, "Yes, sir," or "No, sir," very coldly. She couldn't help it if he did think her dry; if *he* were a little more dry, it might be better for him. What was the matter with him? Oh, she thought she had mentioned that; he was a mesmeric healer, he made miraculous cures.[79]

The repetitions ("she believed he was very bright"/"she supposed he *was* very bright"; "she hadn't read anything"/ "she didn't read much"; "the other that she knew—only she didn't know him"/"she knew him . . . but, she didn't know him"; ". . . he did think her dry"/"if *he* were a little more dry") alone are enough to give the passage the quality of actual speech. The backtracking, stopping, and starting, reinforced here by the hesitations *(well, oh)* and the parentheticals, are typical of ordinary spoken language but are quite different from a written summary of it. In addition to these patterns, we find elliptical constructions ("hadn't read anything"/"not for amusement"/"only the 'Transcript' "), speech level emphasis *("he")*, the use of modals *(would, should, couldn't)*, definite articles that refer to the immediate conversational context ("*the* young man with the 'side-whiskers' "/"*the* tall, pale gentleman"), and a direct question form ("What was the matter with him?"). This question attests to Basil's continuing interest without permitting him an actual interruption.

As directly reported discourse, this little speech would be

79. Ibid., pp. 43–44.

both boring and artificial because it would suggest that it included *all* that Dr. Prance had to say, and with no evidence of Basil's participation, it would be a strangely long discourse for anyone (except perhaps Mrs. Luna!) and particularly for the taciturn Dr. Prance. Moreover, she goes on for some time longer and eventually offers a comment on Verena ("Oh, if she was his child, she would be sure to have some gift . . . if it was only the gift of the g___ well, she didn't mean to say that; but a talent for conversation . . . Yes, she was pretty-appearing, but there was a certain indication of anemia, and Doctor Prance would be surprised if she didn't eat too much candy").[80] Thus, the narrator manages to present, apparently very economically, the meandering patterns of a casual conversation. This use of compact ID reoccurs throughout the novel; elsewhere, it is coupled with an occasional narrator comment or with other more diffused forms of ID.

Reports of characters' thoughts or perceptions are handled in much the same way as speech reports, ranging from the rare direct quote (" 'The delightful girl,' he said to himself; 'she smiles at me as if she liked me!' ")[81] to the tagged and often diffused report (she/he said to/asked her/himself) to untagged compact ID. Minor characters have considerably less reported thought than major characters, but it is remarkable, particularly in Book First, how many of their thoughts are presented. As Putt notes, "minor characters are endowed with a quality of life far in excess of anything required by purely structural considerations."[82]

These thoughts most often are about the major characters and, therefore, simultaneously develop them and the minor characters themselves. For example, shortly before Dr. Prance's monologue the reader is given Miss Birdseye's view of the Tarrants.

80. Ibid., p. 45.
81. Ibid., p. 89.
82. Putt, *Henry James*, p. 188.

Miss Birdseye rested her dim, dry smile upon the daughter, who was new to her, and it floated before her that she
would probably be remarkable as a genius; her parentage
was an implication of that. There was a genius for Miss
Birdseye in every bush. Selah Tarrant had effected wonderful cures; she knew so many people—if they would
only try him. His wife was a daughter of Abraham Green-
street; she had kept a runaway slave in her house for thirty
days. That was years before, when this girl must have
been a child; but hadn't it thrown a kind of rainbow over
her cradle, and wouldn't she naturally have some gift?
The girl was very pretty, though she had red hair.[83]

It becomes obvious as we progress in Book First that Miss
Birdseye is the only character to hold a good opinion of the
elder Tarrants, and the narrator's sarcastic comment on Miss
Birdseye's "genius in every bush" immediately casts doubt on
the validity of her perceptions. (Miss Birdseye is remarkable
in the novel both for her muddleheadedness and the fondness
of all major characters for her.) Although only two portions
of this report are compact—"if they would only try him" and
"but hadn't it thrown a kind of rainbow . . . ?"—the sentiments expressed, aside from the one clear narrator comment,
are Miss Birdseye's. We know this, in part, because of the context—these views contrast so sharply with those of other characters that they cannot be attributed to the narrator *per se*. For
example, when we are permitted a quick look inside the formidable Mrs. Farrinder, "she asked herself whether Miss Tarrant were a remarkable young woman or only a forward minx.
She found a response which committed her to neither view;
she only said, 'We want the young—of course we want the
young!' "[84] The terms used to express Mrs. Farrinder's views
may be her own or narrator summary, but the perspective is
nevertheless hers. (It is interesting that Mrs. Luna calls

83. James, *The Bostonians*, pp. 32–33.
84. Ibid., p. 53.

Verena "an artful little minx"[85] in a stretch of reported discourse that is very clearly compact, making both the terms and the sentiments Mrs. Luna's.)

Reports of minor characters' thoughts are somewhat more obtrusive in Books Second and Third because of the way the narrator comments on them. At the same time, the divisions between narrator comment and indirectly reported discourse become less clear. In describing a conversation between Olive and Mrs. Burrage, the narrator offers a lengthy "justification" for revealing Mrs. Burrage's thoughts:

> If we were this moment to take, in a single glance, an inside view of Mrs. Burrage (a liberty we have not yet ventured on), I suspect we should find that she was considerably exasperated at her visitor's superior tone, at seeing herself regarded by this dry, shy, obstinate, provincial young woman as superficial. If she liked Verena very nearly as much as she tried to convince Miss Chancellor, she was conscious of disliking Miss Chancellor more than she should probably ever be able to reveal to Verena.[86]

The opening commentary draws the reader into the narrative process but distances him from the character herself. Moreover, the narrator's tentativeness ("I suspect we should find") seems overly self-conscious, particularly since we have, in fact, already had an inside view of Mrs. Burrage at her Wednesday Club evening: "She had been on the point of saying it was the reason why he [Basil] was in her house; but she had bethought herself in time that this ought to pass as a matter of course."[87]

As we get into Mrs. Burrage's thoughts on Olive, the narrator strikes an interesting balance between an inside and outside perspective. The narrator wants us to believe that it is

85. Ibid., p. 208.
86. Ibid., p. 319.
87. Ibid., p. 281.

Mrs. Burrage who sees Olive as "dry, shy, obstinate, provincial," but we are not asked to accept these as actual terms she used in her own thoughts. The first clause of the second sentence ("If she liked Verena . . .") would seem to represent the narrator's doubts about Mrs. Burrage's sincerity since Mrs. Burrage herself is quite adamant in her liking, but the second clause once again summarizes Mrs. Burrage's sentiments. A few paragraphs later the narrator engages once again in this balancing act: "Mrs. Burrage—since we have begun to look into her mind we may continue the process—had not meant anyone in particular; but a train of association was suddenly kindled in her thought by the flash of the girl's resentment."[88] Despite the narrator's assertion that we are in Mrs. Burrage's mind, we are, in fact, treated to his "omniscient" summary of her position. The only portion of this summary that truly represents Mrs. Burrage is the reference to Olive as "the girl"; the same pattern emerges in the first passage when Olive is referred to as Miss Chancellor.[89]

Habegger asserts that the narrator's "truly Jamesian self-consciousness about his narrator's point of view"[90] marks a decided shift in Books Second and Third toward a limited point of view. I think rather that the narrator's role itself diminishes as does his distance from his principal characters. He relies more fully on their perceptions and reactions to one another to carry the story. Less space is afforded the reported discourse of minor characters. When these characters do "think" for the reader, the narrator shows a hesitancy about presenting their thoughts omnisciently. For example, in the final scene we get a brief glimpse of Henry Burrage: "It even seemed to occur to him that he might, perhaps, interpose with effect, and he evidently would have liked to say that, without really bragging, *he* would at least have kept the affair from

88. Ibid., p. 330.
89. The way in which the narrator alternates between *Miss Chancellor* and *Olive* in referring to her is provocative and requires further study.
90. Habegger, "The Disunity of *The Bostonians*," p. 204.

turning into a row."[91] The tentative "might, perhaps" represent Henry's thoughts (the emphasis on *he* in the indirect
quote would be his linguistic responsibility), but the narrator
is equally tentative with "it seemed to occur" and "he evidently would."

major characters' indirectly reported discourse

The content of minor characters' reported discourse
often reveals them as fuzzy-thinking or inconsequential. The
dual perspective (that of the narrator and the character) afforded by indirect reports provides ironic distance. Where
ambiguity about linguistic responsibility exists, as it often
does, it is not really significant since the reader is able to separate the "opinion" of the character from that of the narrator.
However, the linguistic ambiguity in indirect reports of Basil,
Olive, and sometimes Verena is significant since at times it
becomes impossible to separate the narrator's position from
that of the major characters.

Such a separation has been the chief preoccupation of many
critical studies of *The Bostonians*. The novel is usually ap-
proached as a social commentary. Therefore, in order to determine James's position on a variety of social issues,[92] one
has to decide which of the two extreme principal characters
(Basil or Olive) James, through his narrator, most sympathizes with. For example, Robert E. Long identifies Ransom
as the hero, "an American European,"[93] and Lionel Trilling

91. James, *The Bostonians*, p. 463.

92. Charles Thomas Samuels summarizes some of these issues: "Olive and Basil
polarize three separate issues. He stands for stoical acceptance; she for an irresponsible commitment to social reform. He stands for normal sexuality; she for 'one of
those friendships between women which are so common in New England'. He stands
for the rights of privacy; she is willing to make an ally of Matthias Pardon" (Charles
Thomas Samuels, *The Ambiguity of Henry James* [Urbana: The University of Illinois
Press, 1971], p. 105).

93. Robert E. Long, "The Society and the Masks: *The Blithedale Romance* and *The
Bostonians,*" *Nineteenth-Century Fiction* 19 (1964): 112.

sees Ransom as a precursor of the modern Southern agrarian.[94] Yet Oscar Cargill finds Ransom overrated as compared to Olive, "a tragic figure."[95] This preoccupation with the narrator's sympathies has led to major misreadings of the novel and of the characters themselves. All three principals are presented in a "gray" light, alternately evoking the reader's sympathy and disdain. If the novel is viewed as a "social commentary," this fuzziness leads inevitably to the conclusion that the novel fails in its primary purpose. The alternative is to distort the characterizations in order to "see" a clarity which is not there. Yet the novel is primarily a study of character and in that sense it is intensely "realistic" since each character is presented with weaknesses and strengths. Cargill's comment on Olive might be extended to the other major characters as well: "It is a tribute to James's skill that the general reaction to her is what it would be in life."[96]

The tensions between the main characters, the sources of those tensions in their personalities, and the less than satisfactory resolution of those tensions are the real subject of the work. Viewed in this way, the novel is far more successful than as an "issue" novel. Its primary flaws lie not in the manipulation of the characters themselves but in the manner of narration, that is, in the actual role of the narrator. It is not so much as Philip Page suggests that "the narrator's treatment of the characters is inconsistent"[97]—these characters have many facets and to present each of them in a consistently favorable or critical light would minimize the complexity of characterization that critics have generally praised in the novel—it is that the narrator's relationship to the characters and to the story itself is inconsistent.

94. Lionel Trilling, *The Opposing Self* (New York and London: Harcourt Brace Jovanovich, 1978), pp. 99–100.

95. Cargill, *The Novels of Henry James*, p. 136.

96. Ibid., p. 137.

97. Philip Page, "The Curious Narration of *The Bostonians*," *American Literature* 24 (1969): 376.

Contrary to the assertions of various critics, the perspective of no one character dominates the novel. Key scenes are presented through Basil's eyes, but he is the outsider and his contact with the other two protagonists comes through these scenes and meetings. Olive's thoughts, on the other hand, are recorded more often than Basil's, and the narrator seems to preserve the least distance from them, but at no time do they serve as the primary means for interpreting the story. Verena, the least-developed central character, has some lengthy sections of reported discourse, but they are sporadic and inconclusive.

The narrator offers subjective and unflattering evaluations of all three characters, particularly in the first half of the novel. He discusses Basil's speech and his choice of words— *Boeotian* as discussed above and *party* in "the 'party,' as he would have said (I cannot pretend that his speech was too heroic for that)."[98] He divorces himself from Basil's "ill-starred views" with specific comments— "(I am but the reporter of his angry *formulae*)"; "his private reflection, colored . . . by 'sectional' prejudice."[99] Olive's extremist and romantic views come under fire: "She liked to think that Verena, in her childhood, had known almost the extremity of poverty, and there was a kind of ferocity in the joy with which she reflected that there had been moments when this delicate creature came near (if the pinch had only lasted a little longer) to literally going without food."[100] Olive's reflection here is ambiguous. "The delicate creature" would seem to be compact ID, but the parenthetical is probably a narrator comment. The narrator frequently points to Olive's faulty logic which enables her to create objective explanations for outcomes that satisfy her personal desires.

98. James, *The Bostonians*, p. 214.
99. Ibid., pp. 194, 50, and 45.
100. Ibid., p. 112.

Olive considered all this, as it was her effort to consider everything, from a very high point of view, and ended by feeling sure it was not for the sake of any nervous personal security that she desired to see her two relations in New York get mixed up together. If such an event as their marriage would gratify her sense of fitness, it would be simply as an illustration of certain laws. Olive, thanks to the philosophic cast of her mind, was exceedingly fond of illustrations of laws.[101]

The narrator mocks Verena's self-centeredness: ". . . she [Verena] quite agreed with her companion [Olive] that after so many ages of wrong (it would also be after the European journey) men must take *their* turn, men must pay!"[102] Again, by using indirectly reported thought, the narrator's satire in this passage becomes ambiguous. The emphasis *("their")* and the exclamation are presumably Verena's responsibility, but the aside about the European trip might be either the narrator's or Verena's. As the narrator's sarcastic comment on Verena's practical, non-idealistic sources of pleasure, it undermines the idealistic momentum of the entire passage. If Verena actually says this as an aside, she appears calculating and somewhat callous.

Conversations with Verena provide an occasion for recording the indirect speech of both "manipulating" characters. In Book First a long indirectly reported speech of Olive's casts considerable light on Olive's perception of herself and contributes as well to later plot developments.

Some weeks later she explained to Verena how definite this pre-vision had been, how it had filled her all day with a nervous agitation so violent as to be painful. She told her that such forebodings were a peculiarity of her organization, that she didn't know what to make of them, that she had to accept them; and she mentioned, as another

101. Ibid., p. 164.
102. Ibid., p. 186.

example, the sudden dread that had come to her the evening before in the carriage, after proposing to Mr. Ransom to go with her to Miss Birdseye's. This had been as
strange as it had been instinctive, and the strangeness, of
course, was what must have struck Mr. Ransom; for the
idea that he might come had been hers, and yet she suddenly veered round. She couldn't help it; her heart had
begun to throb with the conviction that if he crossed that
threshold some harm would come of it for her. She hadn't
prevented him, and now she didn't care, for now, as she
intimated, she had the interest of Verena, and that made
her indifferent to every danger, to every ordinary pleasure. By this time Verena had learned how peculiarly her
friend was constituted, how nervous and serious she was,
how personal, how exclusive, what a force of will she had,
what a concentration of purpose.[103]

This report has certain characteristics in common with the
lengthy indirectly reported speeches of minor characters.
Olive is much taken up with her subject; Verena has no role
in this conversation aside from passive listener. Verena's reaction to the speech—the narrator's summary of Verena's
knowledge of Olive in the last sentence—indicates its momentum and force. A breathless, run-on quality, particularly
in the second sentence with its cumulative *that* clauses, may
remind the reader of Mrs. Luna's bulldozer effect. But Olive's
speech is intense; there is nothing vague or meandering in
her presentation. She has thought through the "peculiarity
of her organization" and she is able to categorize the events
of her life with regard to it. Like Dr. Prance, Olive is thoughtful, but she is considerably more articulate. The presentation
here moves between compact and diffused ID. The contractions *(couldn't, didn't, hadn't),* the interjections *(of course),* and
the deictic adverb *(now)* are direct discourse features and indicate a compact ID reading for certain sentences. This interpretation is particularly significant for the sentence beginning

103. Ibid., pp. 78–79.

"This had been as strange," because it implies that Olive is aware of her effect on Basil and recognizes the arbitrariness of her behavior ("she couldn't help it . . .").

When Olive offers her thoughts to Verena, little response is necessary from Verena since their views are harmonious and theirs is a sympathetic relationship. Basil's conversations with Verena arouse considerably more response from her. Aside from a few conversations with Mrs. Luna, his talks with Verena are his only opportunity to air his opinions—his "ill-starred views."[104] On their excursion in Central Park in Book Second the reader gets Basil's discourse reported indirectly through Verena:

> As she sat there beside him she thought of some of these things, asked herself whether they were what he was thinking of when he said, for instance, that he was sick of all the modern cant about freedom and had no sympathy with those who wanted an extension of it. What was needed for the good of the world was that people should make a better use of the liberty they possessed. Such declarations as this took Verena's breath away; she didn't suppose you could hear anyone say such a thing as that in the nineteenth century, even the least advanced. It was of a piece with his denouncing the spread of education; he thought the spread of education a gigantic farce— people stuffing their heads with a lot of empty catchwords that prevented them from doing their work quietly and honestly. You had a right to an education only if you had an intelligence, and if you looked at the matter with any desire to see things as they are you soon perceived that an intelligence was a very rare luxury, the attribute of one person in a hundred. He seemed to take a pretty low view of humanity, anyway. Verena hoped that something really bad had happened to him—not by way of gratifying any resentment he aroused in her nature, but to help herself to forgive him for so much contempt and brutality.[105]

104. Ibid., p. 194.
105. Ibid., p. 336.

The clause beginning "that he was sick of all the modern cant" may be Verena's exact rendering of Basil's direct discourse or a summary of a number of his ideas. The opinions are certainly his and it seems likely that the wording is as well. The second sentence, however, seems more likely to be Basil's since the narrator refers to it as a "declaration." The sentence is embeddable, but the absence of an introductory tag is the narrator's cue that we are slipping into Basil's own words, albeit filtered through Verena *and* a narrator. The same pattern seems to hold for the fifth sentence. The "you" there is rhetorical—a conversational substitute for "one." The sentence itself is discursive and seems far more like a direct account of the speaker, Basil, than a summary of his position by either Verena or the narrator. Because Basil's views are presented through other characters, their significance would seem to lie not in the philosophy they express but in the effect they have on the listener. The manner of their presentation, as well as the narrator's occasional deprecating asides on their content, makes it unlikely that Ransom is in any way a spokesman for the author, James, or more importantly, that the reader is supposed to take his opinions as major social comments. Rather they reveal his motivation with respect to other key characters.

Because of her filtering role, reflecting the views of the dominant personalities around her, Verena seems to have no life of her own, at least until Book Third. Moreover, all of her public presentations except one, her informal second talk at Miss Birdseye's that the narrator summarizes,[106] come to the reader through Basil's eyes. In the first report, Basil summarizes the content of her talk in a number of ways: "he was the stiffest of conservatives and his mind was steeled against the inanities she uttered—the rights and wrongs of women, the equality of the sexes, the hysterics of conventions, the further stultification of the suffrage, the

106. Ibid., p. 184.

prospect of conscript mothers in the national Senate."[107] But he also thinks "how pretty, indeed, she made some of it sound!" and then launches into the directly reported discourse with which "the young lady finished her harangue."[108] Portions of her speech at the Wednesday Club in New York are also directly reported, but they are prefaced by an interesting counterpoint in which Basil's comments are woven into her speech.

> Certain phrases took on a meaning for him—an appeal she was making to those who still resisted the beneficent influence of the truth. They appeared to be mocking, cynical men, mainly; many of whom were such triflers and idlers, so heartless and brainless that it didn't matter much what they thought on any subject; if the old tyranny needed to be propped up by *them* it showed it was in a pretty bad way. But there were others whose prejudice was stronger and more cultivated, pretended to rest upon study and argument. To those she wished particularly to address herself; she wanted to waylay them, to say, "Look here, you're all wrong; you'll be so much happier when I have convinced you. Just give me five minutes," she should like to say; "just sit down here and let me ask a simple question. Do you think any state of society can come to good that is based upon an organized wrong?" That was the simple question that Verena desired to propound, and Basil smiled across the room at her with an amused tenderness as he gathered that she conceived it to be a poser. He didn't think it would frighten him much if she were to ask him that, and he would sit down with her for as many minutes as she liked.
>
> He, of course, was one of the systematic scoffers, one of those to whom she said—"Do you know how you strike me? You strike me as men who are starving to death while

107. Ibid., p. 62.
108. Ibid., pp. 62 and 63.

they have a cupboard at home, all full of bread and meat and wine. . . ."[109]

The linguistic responsibility for parts of this report is hopelessly ambiguous, but the ambiguity has a purpose. Basil understands what Verena is trying to say and can rise to the challenge she offers, although his attitude continues to be condescending. However, it is unclear whether the terms of the argument as presented here are Verena's or Basil's summary of Verena. Even responsibility for some of the direct discourse is muddled. The context in which the reported information occurs, coupled with our knowledge of how these two characters ordinarily sound, are the only means available to sort out the ambiguity. For example, "the beneficent influence of the truth" must be Basil's summary both because it is removed structurally from any direct discourse and because it sounds like Basil's flowery, often deprecating, phraseology. The first half of the second sentence continues to be summary, but beginning after the semicolon we seem to move closer to Verena's words with the somewhat colloquial "propped up"/"pretty bad way" and the emphasis on "*them.*" It would seem that Verena distinguishes those with a 'cultivated' prejudice since she expresses a desire to address them particularly, at least according to Basil. The double tags on the directly reported discourse that follows ("she wanted . . . to say"/"she should like to say") would seem to reinforce the fact that she does, in fact, say what is quoted; however, the quote may also be Basil's version of her wish, particularly since he takes the address rather personally. The questions in the next two direct quotes are more clearly Verena's. What is lost in this ambiguity is a clear sense of Verena or at least a perspective from which the reader can take her seriously. But the ambiguity conveys very effectively Verena's impact on Basil and her power to engage him despite his antipathy to her views.

109. Ibid., p. 272.

In the indirectly reported thoughts of the major characters we find some of the most tantalizing ambiguities of the novel and some of the most interesting intermingling of narrator and character voices. The ambiguity results in part from the many ways the narrator introduces us to his characters' thoughts. Not only do they "ask" and "say" things to themselves, they also "see," "feel," etc.; variations such as these inevitably blur the distinctions between perspective and actual linguistic responsibility.

Crucial scenes in Book First seem to be reflected through Basil and at the same time controlled by the narrator. A number of critics have commented on the oddity of the following passage:

> . . . at the end of ten minutes Ransom became aware that the whole audience—Mrs. Farrinder, Miss Chancellor, and the tough subject from Mississippi—were under the charm. I speak of ten minutes, but to tell the truth the young man lost all sense of time. He wondered afterwards how long she had spoken; then he counted that her strange, sweet, crude, absurd, enchanting improvisation must have lasted half an hour.[110]

Like numerous descriptions of thought-processes throughout the novel, this one begins with narrator summary and seems to progress through diffused to compact ID. The transitions are by no means clear-cut, but the first sentence summarizes a perception of Basil's with no attempt to use the words he might have used to himself. Ransom views the crowd and recognizes its intensity and preoccupation, but presumably the narrator summarizes the effect on him and calls him "the tough subject from Mississippi." (The narrator may intend to be ironic by suggesting that this is the way Basil actually thinks of himself!) The second sentence, with the "I" of the narrator, is clearly summary but it plays on the subjec-

110. Ibid., p. 61.

tivity of a character's perceptions. The narrator speaks "of ten minutes," but he is merely reporting Basil's awareness, which is unreliable. With the phrase "to tell the truth," the narrator paradoxically excuses himself for having misled the reader and promises that he is now giving honest information. He questions his own omniscience while insisting on it! The last sentence is equally confusing. The adjectives used to describe the speech reflect sentiments we know to be Basil's but not necessarily the narrator's. The subjective modal "must have" again throws the calculation of time into question, and the reader has been led to believe at this point that the narrator does know how long the speech lasted. (Of course, he may only know how long it seemed to Basil to last.) The same ambiguity occurs in Basil's other thoughts on Verena.

The day after Verena's presentation at Mrs. Burrage's Wednesday Club, Basil speculates on Verena's talents.

> Who wouldn't pay half a dollar for such an hour as he had passed at Mrs. Burrage's? The sort of thing she [Verena] was able to do, to say, was an article for which there was more and more demand—fluent, pretty, third-rate palaver, conscious or unconscious perfected humbug; the stupid, gregarious, gullible public, the enlightened democracy of his native land, could swallow unlimited drafts of it.[111]

Because the contemptuous description of Verena's speeches is preceded by a sentence heavily weighted with DD features, the description is meant to be taken as Basil's linguistic responsibility. Moreover, we learn Basil's views on "his native land" elsewhere, and this is a fair statement of them. Therefore, context, content, and actual linguistic organization combine to give the reader Basil's words as nearly as possible without quoting him directly. Since, aside from Mrs. Luna, Basil has no one to discuss these views with, the narrator's

111. Ibid., p. 328.

choices as to the manner of presentation are somewhat limited. He could summarize them completely with little or no hint of Basil's own phraseology or he could use interior monologue which would be much less easy to integrate than compact ID. The continuous presence of the narrator coupled with his skill in moving from his own narrative voice (DN) to compact ID gives the reader generous insights into each major character while permitting him a distance that interior monologue would erase.

In many instances, the characters' perceptions explain their actions. At Miss Birdseye's, Olive as well as Basil views the scene.

> The barren, gas-lighted room grew richer and richer to her earnest eyes; it seemed to expand, to open itself to the great life of humanity. The serious, tired people, in their bonnets and overcoats, began to glow like a company of heroes. Yes, she would do something, Olive Chancellor said to herself; she would do something to brighten the darkness of that dreadful image that was always before her, and against which it seemed to her at times that she had been born to lead a crusade—the image of the unhappiness of women. The unhappiness of women! The voice of their silent suffering was always in her ears, the ocean of tears that they had shed from the beginning of time seemed to pour through her own eyes. Ages of oppression had rolled over them; uncounted millions had lived only to be tortured, to be crucified. They were her sisters, they were her own, and the day of their delivery had dawned. This was the only sacred cause; this was the great, the just revolution. It must triumph, it must sweep everything before it; it must exact from the other, the brutal, blood-stained, ravening race, the last particle of expiation! It would be the greatest change the world had seen; it would be a new era for the human family, and the names of those who had helped to show the way and lead the squadrons would be the brightest in the tables of fame. They would

be names of women weak, insulted, persecuted, but devoted in every pulse to their being to the cause, and asking no better fate than to die for it. It was not clear to
this interesting girl in what manner such a sacrifice (as
this last) would be required of her, but she saw the matter through a kind of sunrise-mist of emotion which
made danger as rosy as success.[112]

As in the passages already discussed, this description opens
with narrator summary of Olive's perceptions. Beginning in
the third sentence we move from her perspective to her actual
voice. The subjective semantics of *yes*, the modal *would*, and
the tag "Olive said to herself" following the assertion identify the clause as Olive's and there is no reason to assume that
the parallel and expanded construction following the semicolon—"she would do something to brighten"—is not also
hers. However, her assertions require some explanation that
would not be necessary to her own thought-process and thus
involve an interesting mingling of narrator and character
voices. It seems at least possible that it is the narrator who
describes "that dreadful image that was always before her,
and against which it seemed to her at times that she had been
born to lead a crusade." But the exclamation of sentence
three and the rhetorical assertions following four seem to express as directly as possible the "sunrise-mist of emotion"
that rolls over Olive at moments such as these. The last sentence is very clearly the narrator's comment; his reference to
Olive as "this interesting girl" distances us from her. The narrator is clearly disparaging Olive's romanticism, and his rendering of the words she might actually have used is the most
effective way to display her views as cliché-ridden and romantic, albeit sincere and intense.

Later in the novel, when Olive's thoughts become more
personal and less abstract, we find this same blend of various
forms of indirect discourse coupled with direct narrator com-

112. Ibid., pp. 37–38.

ment, although the latter is considerably more subtle and less foregrounded. The narrator's role is complicated because he is largely uncritical. In fact, he is on occasion almost sympathetic as he describes the overwhelming nature of Olive's crisis. "From Olive's condition during these lamentable weeks there is a certain propriety—a delicacy enjoined by the respect for misfortune—in averting our head."[113] The narrator often seems to engage in an unspoken dialogue with Olive, posing questions that may have occurred to her and that lead the reader to experience the intensity of Olive's plight. "Did she say to herself that their [women's] weakness was not only lamentable but hideous—hideous their predestined subjection to man's larger and grosser insistence? . . . These are mysteries into which I shall not attempt to enter, speculations with which I have no concern. . . ."[114] The narrator's comment on his lack of concern is misleading since he raises the speculations himself, and in so doing he actively collaborates in the articulation of Olive's thought—a liberty he does not take with the other characters. Moreover, in posing questions for Olive, he adopts her vocabulary and her perspective without the slightest note of mockery or condescension. It would seem then that if a case were to be made for the narrator's sympathies, the evidence weighs equally if not more heavily in favor of Olive than Basil based on the narrator's role in the text.

A subtle passage involving this interesting narrator role describes Olive and Verena's state shortly after Basil arrives in Marmion.

> That was one of the singular speeches that Verena made in the course of their constant discussion of the terrible question, and it must be confessed that she made a great many. The strangest of all was when she protested, as she

113. Ibid., p. 392.
114. Ibid., p. 422.

did again and again to Olive, against the idea of their seeking safety in retreat. She said there was a want of dignity in it—that she had been ashamed, afterwards, of what she had done in rushing away from New York. This care for her moral appearance was, on Verena's part, something new; inasmuch as, though she had struck that note on previous occasions—had insisted on its being her duty to face the accidents and alarms of life—she had never erected such a standard in the face of a disaster so sharply possible. It was not her habit either to talk or to think about her dignity, and when Olive found her taking that tone she felt more than ever that the dreadful, ominous, fatal part of the situation was simply that now, for the first time in all the history of their sacred friendship, Verena was not sincere. She was not sincere when she told her that she wanted to be helped against Mr. Ransom—when she exhorted her, that way, to keep everything that was salutary and fortifying before her eyes. Olive did not go so far as to believe that she was playing a part and putting her off with words which, glossing over her treachery, only made it more cruel; she would have admitted that that treachery was as yet unwitting, that Verena deceived herself first of all, thinking she really wished to be saved. Her phrases about her dignity were insincere, as well as her pretext that they must stay to look after Miss Birdseye: as if Doctor Prance were not abundantly able to discharge that function and would not be enchanted to get them out of the house![115]

The narrator's opening comment is interesting because of the apparently nonironic use of *terrible* and the strange comment "it must be confessed" which admits to many interpretations, none entirely satisfactory. The narrator may be announcing his unwillingness to pry; he may be gently condemning Verena's desire to "talk away" the problem; he may be commenting on the strain of the situation. In the second sentence he makes a value judgment, "strangest of all," that

115. Ibid., pp. 387–88.

seems to ally him very closely to Olive's perspective. The indirect report of Verena's speech in sentence three seems to bear some relation to what she actually said because the later reference to *dignity* makes it likely that she used that word. Sentence four evaluates the situation in a way that only Olive or an omniscient narrator could. The narrator reaffirms the seriousness of the situation—"disaster so sharply possible" —while perhaps mildly chiding Verena for her hypocrisy.

Only in sentence five do we move definitely into Olive's thoughts. This sentence goes from DN to diffused ID to compact ID. "Olive felt" introduces Olive's own thoughts but there are not enough linguistic features in the sentence (before *now*) to classify it as compact ID. "Dreadful, ominous, fatal" would seem to capture Olive's feelings, but, given the narrator's sympathetic involvement, they may be his responsibility. Two elements in the sentence signal compact ID—the temporal *now* and the final clause "she was not sincere." This last clause is echoed at the beginning of the next sentence and again in the last sentence—"her phrases about her dignity were insincere."

In the seventh sentence we encounter the passage's important ambiguity. If Olive does not believe that Verena is "playing a part," then the narrator raises the possibility of "her [Verena's] treachery." Even more problematic is the fact that were Olive to be confronted with "that treachery" she would label it "unwitting." By stepping out of Olive's direct thoughts and suggesting the possibility that Verena is actually duplicitous, the narrator makes the situation more serious while at the same time casting some doubt on both Verena and her motivations and Olive and her honesty with herself. We simply do not know whom to believe. Yet the remainder of the passage weighs heavily against Verena.

There are far fewer instances of Verena's reported thought than of Basil's and Olive's. Her longest and most interesting indirectly reported thoughts come in Book Third when she is most intensely torn between Olive and Basil.

With her light, bright texture, her complacent responsiveness, her genial, graceful, ornamental cast, her desire to
keep on pleasing others at the time when a force she had
never felt before was pushing her to please herself, poor
Verena lived in these days in a state of moral tension—
with a sense of being strained and aching—which she
didn't betray more only because it was absolutely not in
her power to look desperate. An immense pity for Olive
sat in her heart, and she asked herself how far it was necessary to go in the path of self-sacrifice. Nothing was
wanting to make the wrong she should do her complete;
she had deceived her up to the very last; only three
months earlier she had reasserted her vows, given her
word, with every show of fidelity and enthusiasm. There
were hours when it seemed to Verena that she must really
push her inquiry no further, but content herself with the
conclusion that she loved as deeply as a woman could love
and that it didn't make any difference. She felt Olive's
grasp too clinching, too terrible. She said to herself that
she should never dare, that she might as well give up early
as late; that the scene, at the end, would be something
she couldn't face; that she had no right to blast the poor
creature's whole future. She had a vision of those dreadful
years; she knew that Olive would never get over the disap-
pointment. It would touch her in the point where she felt
everything most keenly; she would be incurably lonely
and eternally humiliated. It was a very peculiar thing,
their friendship; it had elements which made it probably
as complete as any (between women) that had ever exist-
ed. Of course it had been more on Olive's side than on
hers; she had always known that; but that, again, didn't
make any difference. It was of no use for her to tell herself
that Olive had begun it entirely and she had only responded out of a kind of charmed politeness, at first, to
a tremendous appeal. She had lent herself, given herself,
utterly, and she ought to have known better if she didn't
mean to abide by it.[116]

116. Ibid., pp. 398–99.

This passage gives the reader a brief glimpse into Verena's motivations, and depending upon whether it is read largely as DN or as ID, it suggests a depth to Verena's self-understanding that does not appear elsewhere. The narrator distances himself considerably more from Verena than he does from Olive in the preceding passage, and his reporting role is less ambiguous. The passage opens with DN–a generous, discursive summary of "poor Verena's" personality and present plight. The reported thought in sentence two begins as a summary of Verena's thoughts and becomes more compact, thus following the pattern of other passages. The halting syntax of the sentence beginning "she said to herself" evokes Verena's actual voice moving toward compact ID.

In fact, our sense of being inside Verena's thoughts, close to interior monologue, continues until the sentence "it was a very peculiar thing, their friendship. . . ." Syntactically, this would seem to be compact ID because of the extraposition of *it*, suggesting a momentary disjunction in thought, and the pause signalled by the comma, before "their friendship." The context reinforces this impression since the sentence is preceded and followed by what seems to be compact ID ("Of course" and "she had always known this"). Yet, it is a strangely dispassionate observation to make in the midst of her mental anguish, and the parenthetical "(between women)" is out of character for Verena but might have occurred to the narrator. This sentence is the most ambiguous in the passage and strongly suggests narrator intrusion. By contrast, the alternative proposed in the sentence "it was no use for her to tell herself," seems to be in the narrator's voice but it is not nearly so ambiguous as the hypothesis presented in the preceding passage on Olive, because it seems apparent from the context here that Verena has actively considered this means of absolving herself and rejected it.

The indirectly reported discourse of the major characters involves some very interesting technical complications. Not only does the narrator's voice mingle with the characters' speech/thought, but characters offer reports of one another.

The reader comes to feel that it is not the substance of the thoughts or speeches themselves that is significant but the impact they have on the characters. The problem, of course, is that the method of reporting often makes the substance and occasionally the impact unclear. The narrator maintains his distance from the major characters by keeping his perspective and voice distinct in Book First. As the perspectives of the major characters become more prominent in the last half of the novel, the narrator's distance from them diminishes. This blurring is most pronounced in reports of Olive's thoughts, and the pattern may be indicative of the narrator's growing sympathy for Olive. Yet she never really becomes the "central consciousness" for the novel, because our sense of her reliability is undermined by the narrator's pity for her.

Although the narrative technique of *The Bostonians* involves some special problems of focus, it manifests difficulties inherent in James's technique and those of the other realists. In a sense, the novel encompasses two approaches to realism. The "Balzatian" narrator of Book First, who " 'goes behind' right and left," achieves a "solidity of specification" with a panorama of characters and events ordered and controlled by his insights and judgments. The narrator's qualifications and hesitations, which in no way diminish his control, make him more personal and trustworthy—more human, in short. This section of the novel conforms to Douglas Hewitt's explanation of realism: "Realistic novels, in short, do not affect us as being like life: they are like the experience of being told about life by someone whom we trust."[117]

As the narrator becomes more involved with his characters, more interested in their perspectives, more dependent upon their voices, his voice becomes more impersonal with respect to the reader. James thus intensifies the reader's experience

117. Douglas Hewitt, *The Approach to Fiction: Good and Bad Readings of Novels* (London: Longman, 1972), p. 55.

by requiring him to confront the complexity involved in the relationships of the characters to one another and to the moral issues central to those relationships. Presenting this complexity without the reassuring presence of a trustworthy guide was another key element in James's theory of realism. Wayne Booth neatly summarizes James's views: "There can be no intensity of illusion if the author is present, constantly reminding us of his unnatural wisdom. Indeed, there can be no illusion of life where there is no bewilderment . . . and the omniscient narrator is obviously not bewildered."[118]

In *The Bostonians* James's narrator sees around his characters while gradually coming to see through their perspectives. In his later fiction, James relies more on a central character's perspective, which accounts for his development of and increasing reliance on forms of indirect discourse. Yet, James's commitment to a "center of knowing," as Morrison has described it,[119] within the consciousness of a character was always tempered by the control of a narrative voice, no matter how unobtrusive. His rejection of first-person narration, involving the first-person of a character not of a narrator external to the story, must be attributed in part to his unwillingness to relinquish this control. In works where he does use the "figural" first-person, for example *The Turn of the Screw,* the reader is often left to question the narrator's credibility, to wonder about his/her reliability, to use Booth's term. James's famous pronouncement that "the house of fiction has . . . not one window, but a million . . ." involves an important qualification:

> The spreading field, the human scene, is the "choice of subject"; the pierced aperture, either broad or balconied or slit-like and low-browed, is the "literary form"; but

118. Wayne Booth, *The Rhetoric of Fiction* (Chicago: University of Chicago Press, 1961), p. 45.

119. Sister Kristen Morrison, "James's and Lubbock's Differing Points of View," *Nineteenth-Century Fiction* 16 (1961): 253.

> they are, singly or together, as nothing without the posted
> presence of the watcher—without, in other words, the
> consciousness of the artist.[120]

That watcher may adopt his character's angle of vision as the
"form" or window, but it is his voice that controls this presentation. When his voice mingles with those of his characters,
the resulting ambiguity can generate healthy, "realistic" bewilderment or the kind of confusion we encounter in *The Bostonians*.

Although the narrator of *The Bostonians* fulfills both representational and interpretive functions, in the second half of
Book Second and all of Book Third, he speaks with less authority and his intrusions are less judgmental than in Book
First. In short, he moves from commentator to observer. Simultaneously, the thoughts and speeches of the three main
characters become more prominent. This shift in focus provides an interpretation for James's comment quoted earlier,
labeling "the middle part . . . too descriptive and explaining
and expatiating." The narrator, in James's view, may continue
to be too prominent and the presentation of the psychological
processes of the characters not dramatic enough.

However, because the narrator is initially critical of both
Basil and Olive, the reader can take neither of them as a satisfying "center of knowing," when confronted with their perspectives. Since the narrator's opinion of each becomes less
clear as the novel progresses, the reader's sympathies are
never fully engaged. The narrator abdicates his external, rhetorical perspective without offering an adequate substitute in
the consciousness of one of the characters. The effect differs
from that of a novel like *The Ambassadors*. There the reader
is never sure how accurate Strether's perceptions are, but the
reader, through the narrator, is committed to Strether's per-

120. Henry James, *The Art of the Novel: Critical Prefaces*, intro. by Richard Blackmur
(New York: Charles Scribner's Sons, 1962), p. 46.

spective from the outset. The narrator sees through the character while gradually allowing the reader to see around him. James's experiment in *The Bostonians* results in an interesting but unsatisfactory objectivity; we are able to see the motivations of each character, as well as their strengths and weaknesses, without having a great sympathy in any one direction.

In *The Rise of Silas Lapham,* the narrator "deals away" his powers by proclaiming his limitations and maintains his objectivity by keeping his voice separate from those of his characters. Yet Howells gets himself into a dilemma similar to James's. The narrator permits Silas' voice and perspective to become more prominent in the latter part of the novel, but, unlike James's narrator, he reins in this growing sympathy when it threatens his "objectivity." The reader, whose sympathy for Silas has grown along with the narrator's, is brought up short. In *Huck Finn*, Twain finds a first-person narrator/ character, a "realistic" voice, who can make an honest claim to antiomniscience but who must also struggle to maintain control of his story.

3
the
rise
of
silas
lapham:
controlled
drama

William Dean Howells wrote *The Rise of Silas Lapham* at the height of his career and in the midst of his aesthetic battle for realism in fiction. Most critics agree that it is Howells' finest novel. It is certainly representative of the technique and subject matter for which he is noted. So passionately involved was Howells in his campaign for realism when he wrote *Silas Lapham* that he incorporates a number of his arguments into the novel itself. As Kermit Vanderbilt notes: "Howells' growing warfare against the sentimental and improbable in fiction led him to the obtrusive literary polemics in *Silas Lapham*."[1] Thus the Reverend Sewell, taken by some to be Howells' moral spokesperson in the novel, comments at the climactic dinner party: " 'The novelists might be the greatest possible help to us if they

1. Kermit Vanderbilt, *The Achievement of William Dean Howells* (Princeton: Princeton University Press, 1968), p. 132.

painted life as it is, and human feelings in their true proportion and relation, but for the most part they have been and are altogether noxious.' "[2] And the character who epitomizes good taste and the artistic temperament, Bromfield Corey, comments further: " 'The commonplace is just that light, impalpable, aërial essence which they've never got in their confounded books yet. The novelist who could interpret the common feelings of commonplace people would have the answer to 'the riddle of the painful earth' on his tongue.' "[3]

Though to modern readers the business problems of a self-made millionaire and his family's difficulties with Boston society may seem rather removed from the "commonplace," for Howells' readers, these were mundane, tame subjects to find in a novel. More important than the subjects themselves was their presentation. There is the potential for tragedy and romance and more importantly for romanticized tragedy in the coplots, as Vanderbilt describes them.[4] But Howells attempted to present these characters as they would appear in real life, scrupulously avoiding the sentimental and the extravagant and allowing the novel's impact to evolve from the characterization.

This "realism" of presentation stirred critical debate over the work, particularly when it was first published. The question arose as to whether these were suitable fictional characters (a corollary question involved whether the conclusion was suitably uplifting), and more importantly for this study, whether they were portrayed in a way that engaged the reader's sympathy. In summarizing hostile criticism, Walter Meserve explains Howells' dilemma by saying "because he did not color his view of life with their preconceived sentimental approach, critics concluded that Howells had no feel-

2. William Dean Howells, *The Rise of Silas Lapham,* intro. and notes to the Text by Walter J. Meserve, Text established by Walter J. Meserve and David J. Nordloh (Bloomington and London: Indiana University Press, 1971), p. 197.

3. Ibid., p. 202.

4. Vanderbilt, *Achievement of Howells,* p. 134.

ing for his people."[5] In fact, Howells' narrator does maintain a distance from all of his characters, including Silas, that might be interpreted as unsympathetic.

Kolb comments that "in spite of his faults and his lack of heroic stature, Silas—like other protagonists in realistic fiction—enlists our sympathy and our respect partly because we get to know him so well."[6] In *The Bostonians* the reader sees Olive's faults, but the narrator offers her the sympathy of thinking through her problems with her. Although Howells knows Silas well and displays his personality fully, his narrator remains aloof.[7] When the narrator becomes involved in the articulation of Silas' problems, he pulls back. Howells' own defense of James (1882) might stand as an explanation of his portrayal of Silas: ". . . that artistic impartiality which puzzled so many in the treatment of Daisy Miller is one of the qualities most valuable in the eyes of those who care how things are done . . . As 'frost performs the effect of fire,' this impartiality comes at last to the same result as sympathy."[8] Familiarity breeds sympathy not contempt.

Howells chose the most difficult mode of narration for his purposes; he seeks "realism" in his portrayals without limiting his narrator to a single perspective or to the perspectives of a small number of characters. In his essay "Novel-Writing and Novel-Reading: An Impersonal Explanation" (1899), Howells uses narrative form to identify three novel "shapes."[9] Of the three shapes, autobiographical, biographical, histori-

5. Walter J. Meserve, Introduction to *The Rise of Silas Lapham* (Bloomington and London: Indiana University Press, 1971), p. xxv.

6. Harold H. Kolb, Jr., *The Illusion of Life: American Realism as a Literary Form* (Charlottesville: The University Press of Virginia, 1969), p. 89.

7. There is no discernible distance between the author and narrator of *Silas Lapham*. As in *The Bostonians,* the narrator records the story and the author or "implied" author shapes the entire novel.

8. William Dean Howells, "Henry James, Jr." (1882) in *W. D. Howells as Critic,* ed. Edwin H. Cady (London and Boston: Routledge & Kegan Paul, 1973), p. 66.

9. William Dean Howells, "Novel-Writing and Novel-Reading: An Impersonal Explanation" ed. William M. Gibson, in *Howells and James: A Double Billing* (New York: The New York Public Library, 1958), p. 22.

cal, Howells labels the historical "the great form, impure and imperfect as it is. . . ."[10] He explains this form as ". . . any sort of novel whose material is treated as if it were real history. In this, the novelist supposes himself to be narrating a series of events, indefinite in compass, and known to him from the original documents, as a certain passage in the real life of the race is known to the historian."[11]

Yet Howells avoids the freedom and flexibility of the historical novelist who "dwells in a world of his own creating, where he is a universal intelligence, comprehending and interpreting everything not indirectly or with any artistic conditions, but frankly and straight-forwardly, without accounting in any way for his knowledge of the facts."[12] Using the realistic technique that Doody describes, Howells is one of the "omniscient authors who make no final claims for their omniscience, who in fact try to disguise or deny it by dealing it away."[13] He tries for an almost objective third-person form, relying heavily on observations of concrete facts and on the directly quoted dialogue of his characters. Kolb notes that Howells is less rigorous than James or Twain in his antiomniscience;[14] however, within the confines of his method of narration, he is, in fact, more rigorous. He is simply less willing to experiment, preferring as he does a more traditional narrative technique.

The narrator of *Silas Lapham* is "objective" and detached to a greater degree than the narrator in either of the other two novels in this study. When Howells allows his narrator rhetorical intrusions in the first person, they are most often generalized observations on the human condition, not relevant directly to the progress or interpretation of the story. The result in terms of narrative form is a potpourri of first- and third-person observation and comment.

10. Ibid., p. 23.

11. Ibid.

12. Ibid.

13. Terrence Doody, *"Don Quixote, Ulysses,* and the Idea of Realism," *Novel* 12 (1979), p. 213.

14. Kolb, *Illusion of Life,* p. 89.

Howells uses every type of discourse in the novel (except unmarked direct), but directly reported discourse is most prominent. In addition, the narrator describes in detail various nonverbal, physical cues. It is interesting in this regard that "during the years immediately prior to and following the writing of *The Rise of Silas Lapham* Howells' interest in writing for the stage was at its highest."[15] As in a play, the characters' speeches and gestures, plus the setting, convey the meaning. Yet despite the narrator's low profile, he appears to be always in control. In this sense, the novel is "authorial" rather than "figural."

narrator's voice

A traditionally "omniscient" narrator is free to comment on and to interpret his characters in the interest of good storytelling. But an obviously manipulative voice detracts from the dramatic presentation that enables the characters to present themselves to the reader. Moreover, the chattier the narrator the less impartial he is likely to be. Howells' narrator is an observer, offering tentative interpretations, but not intervening in the story itself. Yet, his limited omniscience is both too limited and not limited enough. He is not a consistent authoritative voice guiding the reader's perceptions, and his intrusive comments are often distracting. Carrington sees Howells' problem as an inability to "locate" his novels; he neither accepts the responsibility of the narrating "I" nor abandons it altogether.[16]

Characters speak for themselves in *Silas Lapham* and express their opinions of one another. The novel contains much less indirectly reported discourse than either *The Bostonians* or *Huck Finn*. The narrator allows himself only limited access

---

15. Meserve, Introduction to *Silas Lapham*, p. xxvii.
16. George C. Carrington, Jr., *The Immense Complex Drama: The World and Art of the Howells Novel* (Columbus: Ohio State University Press, 1966), p. 196.

to his characters' thoughts and then frequently qualifies this access with a "perhaps" or a "probably." The emphasis on directly reported discourse coupled with narrative reticence prompted James (1886) to a mild criticism: "He has an increasing tendency to tell his story altogether in conversations, so that a critical reader sometimes wishes, not that the dialogue might be suppressed . . . , but that it might be distributed, interspaced with narrative and pictorial matter."[17] James's view contrasts sharply with Twain's appreciation of Howells' "stage directions." Far from finding the narrator's comments on conversations too sparse, Twain (1906) asserts that "sometimes they convey a scene and its conditions so well that I believe I could see the scene and get the spirit and meaning of the accompanying dialogue if some one would read merely the stage directions to me and leave out the talk."[18]

While the characters' discourse carries the story, the author-narrator is never far from the reader's awareness; he is not rigorously effaced from the text. I would not go as far as Carrington who suggests that "in a sense, all of *The Rise of Silas Lapham* is an appendage to comments and generalizations . . . the fiction is inside the essay, which the characters in the fiction know nothing about. . . ."[19] I would agree with Carrington, though, that the novel is replete with Howellsian "comment and generalization."[20] The narrator occasionally

17. Henry James, "William Dean Howells" rpt. in *Howells: A Century of Criticism*, ed. Kenneth E. Eble (Dallas: Southern Methodist University Press, 1967), pp. 49–50. It is interesting to contrast James's view of Howells with Howells on "Mr. Henry James's Later Work" (1903): ". . . I am willing to offer him the reparation of a little detraction. I wish he would leave his people more, not less, to me when I read him. I have tried following their speeches without taking in his comment, delightfully pictorial as that always is, and it seems to me that I make rather more of their meaning, that way" (Howells, *W. D. Howells as Critic*, p. 416).

18. Samuel L. Clemens, "William Dean Howells," (1906) rpt. in *Howells: A Century of Criticism*, p. 86.

19. Carrington, *Immense Complex Drama*, p. 76.

20. Ibid., p. 174. Carrington labels as "generalization" a narrator intrusion that "arises in the course of the narrative and gives it a nudge but does not interrupt it . . . The generalization reminds us of the presence of the hovering narrator, but the momentum of the narrative itself continues almost undisturbed across the brief gap"

offers comments on the characters and their dilemmas, as
when he labels Silas and Mrs. Lapham, "these poor outcasts
of sorrow."[21] He makes some comments in the first person,
"I do not know how it is that clergymen and physicians keep
from telling their wives the secrets confided to them."[22] He
offers personal exclamations about events in the story:
"Heaven knows in what measure the passion of her soul was
mixed with pride. . . ." "Heaven knows how they knew it."[23]
These comments are clearly meant to reinforce the narrator's
role as incredulous observer of actual happenings.

Other narrator intrusions are more digressive and less specifically related to the events of the story. He discusses married life, "the silken texture of the marriage tie bears a daily
strain of wrong and insult which no other human relation can
be subjected to without lesion . . . ," and summers in Boston,
"if you go out of town early, it seems a very long summer
when you come back in October; but if you stay, it passes
swiftly, and seen foreshortened in its flight, seems scarcely a
month's length."[24] These little divergences remind us of the
typical nineteenth-century novel in which ". . . even as the
narrator draws the reader's attention away from the individual fictional character, he fixes it on his own articulate self.
. . ."[25] While the narrator's comments detract from the dramatic presentation, they have little impact on the reader's interpretation of character or theme.

Within his tags on directly reported discourse, the narrator
offers comments on the characters' speech. In fact, although
there is little "dialect" variation recorded in the direct quotations, the speech patterns of the Laphams come in for consid-

(p. 175). He contrasts this type of interruption with longer editorial digressions,
which he labels "comments."

21. Howells, *Silas Lapham*, p. 240.
22. Ibid., p. 362.
23. Ibid., pp. 279 and 315.
24. Ibid., pp. 49 and 126.
25. Dorrit Cohn, *Transparent Minds: Narrative Modes for Presenting Consciousness in Fiction* (Princeton: Princeton University Press, 1978), p. 25.

erable narrative comment. Silas' provincial accent is occasionally cited: "he called it *rud,*" "he said *doos,* of course."[26] When Mr. and Mrs. Lapham discuss the recommendations of the architect, one of which favors " 'the refined Empire style,' " Silas says, " 'I wonder what the Ongpeer style is?' "[27] When the narrator records their casual interchanges indirectly and incorporates some mildly colloquial phrases, he quickly labels them as character responsibility—"as they would have said"; "It seemed to him that he had discovered the fellow (as he always called him)"; "the Colonel . . . was feeling, as he would have said, about right."[28] Finally, the narrator indulges in more sweeping comments about the Laphams' speech: "At times the Colonel's grammar failed him"; "She left her daughter to distribute the pronouns aright."[29] The reader feels pushed to accept Tom Corey's conclusion, " 'But you know that in spite of his syntax I rather liked him?' "[30]

Language is an index of social status and in his comments on their speech, the narrator clearly identifies the Laphams as inferior to the "best" Boston society. The narrator's comments suggest a self-consciousness about the Laphams that makes him anxious to distinguish himself from them. Occasional snobbish asides to the reader reinforce this impression. When the narrator tells us that Mrs. Lapham ". . . passed Irene a cup of Oolong tea—none of them had a sufficiently cultivated palate for Souchong—,"[31] we may admire his attention to detail, quite literally "teacup realism,"[32] while recognizing it as an excuse to put down the Laphams. When the

26. Howells, *Silas Lapham,* pp. 18 and 37.
27. Ibid., pp. 42 and 43.
28. Ibid., pp. 37, 43, and 82.
29. Ibid., pp. 38 and 147.
30. Ibid., p. 65.
31. Ibid., p. 37.
32. Carrington notes that "the term 'teacup realism,' applied to Howells by Frank Norris, a Byronic romantic, suggests a leaden matter-of-factness that does exist in Howells but as a strategy, not as an end in itself" (Carrington, *Immense Complex Drama,* p. 55).

Laphams show up at the Corey dinner party without Penelope, the narrator tells us that "Robert Chase, the painter, had not come, and Mrs. James Bellingham was not there, so that the table really balanced better without Penelope; but Mrs. Lapham could not know this, and did not deserve to know it."[33] The final critical evaluation may reflect Mrs. Corey's opinion, but the narrator does not specifically exclude himself from sharing it. These comments may well reflect Howells' ambiguity about social class. As Vanderbilt notes, "Howells' sentiment toward the average man in America was perhaps like Lowell's . . .—a democracy of the head but not profoundly of the heart."[34] Vanderbilt quotes Howells himself as saying, " 'My convictions were all democratic . . . but at heart I am afraid I was a snob.' "[35]

The narrator for all of his intrusions takes pains to indicate the limitations of his knowledge. The phrase "as if" figures as largely in the tags on directly reported discourse as the adverb *apparently* does in the narrative itself. Carrington notes that "in this novel the author not only uses eleven different terms of uncertainty ('no doubt,' 'doubtless,' 'perhaps,' 'apparently,' 'probably,' 'as if,' 'seemed,' 'must have,' 'it is questionable if,' 'it might almost be said that,' 'and no proof that she meant more'), but on four occasions offers alternative reasons for a character's actions or thoughts."[36] In the opening scene the narrator offers a tentative explanation of one of Lapham's statements: "as if unwilling to give himself too much credit. . . ."[37] In describing Lapham's first meeting with Bromfield Corey, the narrator uses a modal verb qualifier: "that must have been his way of letting Corey see that he was not overcome by the honor of his father's visit."[38] Another

33. Howells, *Silas Lapham*, p. 190.
34. Vanderbilt, *Achievement of Howells*, p. 142.
35. Ibid., p. 107.
36. Carrington, *Immense Complex Drama*, p. 178.
37. Howells, *Silas Lapham*, p. 7.
38. Ibid., p. 144.

qualifier, *no doubt,* comes up on several occasions: "Lapham suffered himself to be persuaded, the more easily, no doubt, because. . . ."[39] The related *doubtless* carries the same effect: ". . . but Penelope was looking at Mrs. Corey, who doubtless saw her from the corner of her eyes. . . ."[40] Finally, we have the frequently occurring *whether*—"Whether she was daunted and confused . . . or whether her perceptions had been blunted . . . it would be difficult to say."[41]

Indications of uncertainty have a more subtle effect when the narrator transmits the perceptions of characters. Thus, for example, the narrator says of Lapham: "He probably thought this a neat, off-hand way of making the invitation . . . ."[42] Only Lapham, not the narrator, thinks his manner is "neat and off-hand," but the narrator isn't absolutely sure of what Lapham thought. An almost parallel passage occurs somewhat later in the novel: "Lapham expanded with profound self-satisfaction. As he probably conceived it, he had succeeded in praising, in a perfectly casual way, the supreme excellence of his paint. . . ."[43] Both reader and narrator know that Lapham's way is anything but casual; therefore, the narrator's description distances the reader from Lapham. But the ironic distance is softened by the narrator's unwillingness to judge absolutely.

The narrator's tentativeness becomes almost coy in the romantic coplot. When he says of Irene that "she clung to the young man's hand an imperceptible moment longer than need be, or else he detained her,"[44] the narrator cannot definitely account for a physical occurrence he observes. If Tom Corey were detaining her, it would indicate an interest that he later denies.

39. Ibid., p. 154.
40. Ibid., p. 167.
41. Ibid., p. 328.
42. Ibid., p. 56.
43. Ibid., p. 141.
44. Ibid., p. 57.

Much of the narrator's subjective vocabulary consists of descriptions of characters' physical attributes and actions. Silas is consistently portrayed as massive and somewhat brutal. In the opening scene, he is said to have a "large head," a "great hairy fist," and a "huge foot." Bromfield Corey is described on several occasions as a "white-mustached old gentleman."[45] When Tom Corey first meets Penelope, the narrator records his impression: he "saw that she was shorter than her sister, and had a dark complexion."[46] Physical appearance not only identifies, it communicates, and kinesic communication is both dramatic and realistic. In describing gestures, glances, and facial expressions, the narrator assumes the role of unbiased observer.

Some nonverbal communication is recorded like direct discourse: "Irene looked, 'I wonder what papa is going to say next!' at her sister. . . ."[47] In a climactic scene in the novel, the narrator describes what Lapham observed:

> It was a deeper game than Lapham was used to, and he sat looking with a sort of admiration from one Englishman to the other, and then to Rogers, who maintained an exterior of modest neutrality, and whose air said, "I have brought you gentlemen together as the friend of all parties, and I now leave you to settle it among yourselves. I ask nothing, and expect nothing, except the small sum which shall accrue to me after the discharge of my obligation to Colonel Lapham."[48]

Most often the characters' direct discourse is augmented with these descriptions. They are either part of the narrator's tag or part of a longer explanation resulting from a character exchange. On the occasion of Tom Corey's first visit to the Laphams at the shore, Penelope and Mrs. Lapham discuss his motives in a lively exchange as Irene "looks on."

45. Ibid., p. 62.
46. Ibid., p. 53.
47. Ibid., p. 56.
48. Ibid., p. 324.

"Well, if you want my candid opinion, I think this talk about business is nothing but a blind. It seems a pity Irene shouldn't have been up to receive him," she added.

Irene cast a mute look of imploring at her mother, who was too much preoccupied to afford her the protection it asked.

"Your father said he wanted to go into business with him."

Irene's look changed to a stare of astonishment and mystification. . . .[49]

Descriptions of physical acts or appearances offer the reader the opportunity to come to conclusions, and they are sometimes coupled with indications of the narrator's uncertainty. The narrator can suggest an interpretation for a phenomenon he observes without insisting on it: "Whether he satisfied himself by this or not, he reddened a little after he had said it"; "Mrs. Corey drew a long breath as if she did not experience the suggested consolation. . . ."[50] When the reader encounters Rogers "shedding tears" in the Lapham living room, we learn "apparently he was not ashamed of them, for the expression with which he met Lapham was that of a man making a desperate appeal in his own cause. . . ."[51] His observable demeanor leads to the conclusion that he is not ashamed.

The reader can never quite escape the narrator in *Silas Lapham,* who is both preoccupied and uneasy with his role. He strains for "objectivity," actually drawing attention to his inability to judge characters and events, but his views come through. Only in the directly reported discourse of the text is he able to achieve the neutrality he professes to value.

49. Ibid., p. 87.
50. Ibid., pp. 60 and 103.
51. Ibid., p. 327.

directly reported discourse

Howells' extensive use of directly reported discourse, much more prominent in *Silas Lapham* than in *Huck
Finn* or *The Bostonians*, supports the dramatic development of
the narrative and the objectivity of the narrator. To a certain
extent the narrator's descriptions and tags, the events of the
story, and some recorded thought shape the reader's view of
the characters. However, we know these characters primarily
through their talk, both the speeches and the qualities attributed to their actual speech patterns by the narrator. Moreover, dialogues reveal much background information,
supplied by the narrator in more traditional novels. In the
opening chapter, Bartley Hubbard's interview of Silas is a
concise and dramatic way of sketching in Silas' financial rise
and familial background with minimal narrator comment.

If Howells' directly reported discourse can be faulted, it is
for its manners not for its appropriateness. Richard Bridgman, who credits Howells as a "real and successful pioneer
in the exploration of middle-class speech,"[52] criticizes his
dialogue for being "prematurely polished, composed, arranged."[53] Thus Howells' characters, except when under
pressure, do not grope for words; their talk does not drift;
they sometimes "speechify." However, Bridgman fails to consider the diversity of Howells' middle-class speech. In some
of their exchanges Anna and Bromfield Corey might be mistaken for Jamesian characters, albeit the Fanny and Colonel
Assingham types; the simple, earnest Laphams remind us of
some of the people Huck encounters. Howells progressed
considerably from the stilted, usually ornamental, dialogue
of his "romantic" predecessors. His directly reported discourse *is* the novel in large part and it rings true for the
reader.

---

52. Richard Bridgman, *The Colloquial Style in America* (New York: Oxford University
Press, 1968), p. 75.
53. Ibid., p. 77.

Because Howells relies so heavily on directly reported discourse, the mode functions in a variety of ways. For example, the narrator uses Bromfield Corey's direct discourse to sketch in Corey's own relationship with his father and to compare it implicitly with his relationship to his son.

> "Well, let us compromise," he seemed to be saying to his father's portrait. "I will travel." "Travel? How long?" the keen eyes demanded. "Oh, indefinitely. I won't be hard on you, father." He could see the eyes soften, and the smile of yielding come over his father's face; the merchant could not resist a son who was so much like his dead mother.[54]

The symbolism—Corey, the painter, talking to his own portrait of his father—is enhanced by the dramatic presentation, as is the poignancy and charm of the scene. Bromfield Corey can either recall or imagine his father's words and his own gentle, self-deprecating wit. The descriptive sentence after the exchange is balanced between Corey's remembrance of his father's face and the narrator's explication of the father's reaction. The narrator is summarizing Corey's own perceptions, but the description—"the merchant," "a son," "his dead mother"—is in the narrator's voice.

Howells' narrator frequently uses direct discourse to provide transitions within and between chapters, as if he were opening and closing scenes. In chapter 9 he provides a sharp contrast between Bromfield Corey, the unhurried aristocrat, and Silas Lapham, the bustling business man, by having them comment consecutively on the same subject, namely, a visit to Lapham by Corey as a consequence of Tom Corey's employment. Tom and his father discuss the subject and their conversation ends: " 'Well,' said the elder, with easy resignation, 'there's at least no hurry.' "[55] Immediately the reader is confronted with:

54. Howells, *Silas Lapham*, p. 70.
55. Ibid., p. 119.

"There is one thing I don't like," said Lapham, in the
course of one of those talks which came up between his
wife and himself concerning Corey, "or at least I don't
understand it; and that's the way his father behaves. I
don't want to force myself on any man; but it seems to
me pretty queer the way he holds off. . . ."[56]

Rather than using the tag for a transition, the narrator
plunges the reader into Silas' grumbling. The tag itself compresses information about the occasion and the fact that Tom
Corey is a frequent topic of Lapham conversation.

Over and above all its other uses, directly reported
discourse enables the characters to create themselves. In
chapter 1, Bartley Hubbard's interview of Silas Lapham
serves several purposes. Bartley sketches in Lapham's appearance, his family background, his business accomplishments;
the dialogue itself and the tags on it reveal Lapham to the
reader as he would appear to a stranger. The reader gets a
sense of Lapham from an objective, somewhat jaded, journal-
ist's point of view. Chapter 2 switches the reader immediately
to the Lapham domestic setting where Silas appears in a different, and, according to Kolb,[57] more sympathetic light. In
chapter 1 Silas has a sense of humor but little irony; he is
shrewd and simple—proud of his accomplishments; he is ag-
gressive but fair.

Lapham opens the interview with the light inquiry " 'so you
want my life, death, and Christian sufferings, do you, young
man?' "[58] Banter carries them to Bartley's suggestion that
Lapham begin with his birth, which prompts "a gleam of humorous appreciation . . . into Lapham's blue eyes" and
launches him into his history. His enthusiasm for America ("I
was bound to be an American of *some* sort, from the word
Go!"), his work (" 'Well, say I'm fifty-five years old, and I've

56. Ibid.
57. Kolb, *Illusion of Life,* p. 88.
58. Howells, *Silas Lapham,* p. 3.

lived 'em, too; not an hour of waste time about *me,* any-wheres!' "), and himself carries him along until Bartley pulls him up by calling his childhood "regulation thing" and in-quires about "any barefoot business" "with a smile of cynical good-camaradery."[59] "Lapham looked at him silently, and then said with quiet self-respect, 'I guess if you see these things as a joke, my life wont inter*est* you.' "[60] Lapham is capa-ble of innocent self-aggrandizement, but his evaluation of his past is sincere, and he resents Bartley's mockery.

Similarly, when Lapham shows Bartley a family picture, he describes his nephew as " 'good-looking.' " Bartley picks out Irene and echoes the description:

> "*She's* a good-looking chap," said Bartley, with prompt irreverence. He hastened to add, at the frown which gath-ered between Lapham's eyes, "What a beautiful creature she is! What a lovely, refined, sensitive face! And she looks *good,* too."
> "She *is* good," said the father, relenting.[61]

In this neat exchange, not only do the participants repeat one another's words with slightly different nuances as they would in ordinary conversation, but they also respond to the tone and manner of the other. The narrator is a recorder; he observes the intonations and the facial expressions and notes them. Later the narrator comments on the photograph; he tells us nothing about the family except how they appear in *this* picture: "The photographer had not been able to conceal the fact that they were all decent, honest-looking, sensible people. . . ."[62]

Throughout the interview the narrator plays off Bartley's biases, recording them to make himself seem more objective. For example, early in the interview the narrator quotes Bart-

59. Ibid., pp. 4 and 5.
60. Ibid.
61. Ibid., p. 8.
62. Ibid.

ley's article in some detail. The article closes with a "gibe"
that "Bartley could not deny himself"—" 'They were quiet,
unpretentious people, religious, after the fashion of that time,
and of sterling morality, and they taught their children the
simple virtues of the Old Testament and Poor Richard's Al-
manac.' " Bartley "trusted to Lapham's unliterary habit of
mind for his security in making it. . . ."[63] Bartley's cynicism
underlines Lapham's simplicity; the narrator merely reports
Bartley's attitude, although he might seem to be judging and
inviting the reader to judge Lapham.

Silas' colloquial speech patterns are more pronounced in
this conversation than anywhere else in the novel, although
some of the patterns he establishes here continue. Both his
pronunciation and word choice are marked for dialect:
"wa'n't," "aint," "tell'em," "m'wife," "Mis' Lapham," "shif
'less," "haint," "aint a-going." When he discusses the paint
itself, "Lapham pronounced the scientific phrases with a sort
of reverent satisfaction, as if awed through his pride by a little
lingering uncertainty as to what peroxide was. He accented
it as if it were purr-ox-*eyed;* and Bartley had to get him to spell
it."[64]

During the interview, Lapham has several long monologues
accounting for his success with his paint, a subject that in-
spires his self-confidence. He includes details largely irrelevant to the story but likely to be part of his memory—" 'I'd
let the place for seventy-five dollars a year to a shif 'less kind
of a Kanuck that had come down that way; and I'd hated to
see the house with him in it. . . ."[65] He is unself-conscious
enough to quote himself and his wife: ". . . and says I, 'What
do you think, Persis?' and says she, 'well, you haint got a
paint-mine, Silas Lapham; you've got a *gold*-mine.' "[66] Not
until he encounters a level of society where he feels unsure

63. Ibid., p. 5.
64. Ibid., p. 11.
65. Ibid., p. 9.
66. Ibid., p. 10.

of himself and to which he aspires does he begin to have self-doubts.

Conversations between Silas and Persis embody the narrator's description of them: "They liked to talk to each other in that blunt way; it is the New England way of expressing perfect confidence and tenderness."[67] Each uses the other person as a sounding board to determine and express his or her own position. They fill in one another's thoughts and understand what is left unsaid, and they converse simply and unpretentiously. Howells' skill with this kind of dialogue is unsurpassed. It is the innovative dialogue that Richard Bridgman describes: "the language is commonplace, relaxed, immediately apprehensible, unpoetic. It lacks metaphor, is commonsensical, businesslike. In its very dryness it embodies the values of the middle class with its idea of social self-effacement."[68]

Early in the novel after Mrs. Corey and her daughters pay the Laphams a visit and comment unfavorably on the part of town where the Laphams live, Silas and Persis discuss the matter.

> "Oh, well, of course," said Lapham, to whom these facts were referred. "Those sort of people haven't got much business up our way, and they don't come. It's a fair thing all round. We don't trouble the Hill or the New Land much."
>
> "We know where they are," suggested his wife, thoughtfully.
>
> "Yes," assented the Colonel. "*I* know where they are. I've got a lot of land over on the Back Bay."
>
> "You have?" eagerly demanded his wife.
>
> "Want me to build on it?" he asked in reply, with a quizzical smile.
>
> "I guess we can get along here for a while."

67. Ibid., p. 32.
68. Bridgman, *Colloquial Style*, p. 76.

This was at night. In the morning Mrs. Lapham said:

"I suppose we ought to do the best we can for the children, in every way."

"I supposed we always had," replied her husband.

"Yes, we have, according to our light."

"Have you got some new light?"

"I don't know as it's light. But if the girls are going to keep on living in Boston and marry here, I presume we ought to try to get them into society, some way; or ought to do something."

"Well, who's ever done more for their children than we have?" demanded Lapham, with a pang at the thought that he could possibly have been outdone. "Don't they have everything they want? Don't they dress as you say? Don't you go everywhere with 'em? Is there ever anything going on that's worthwhile that they don't see it or hear it? *I* don't know what you mean. Why don't you get them into society? There's money enough!"

"There's got to be something besides money, I guess," said Mrs. Lapham, with a hopeless sigh. "I presume we didn't go to work just the right way about their schooling. We ought to have got them into some school where they'd have got acquainted with city girls—girls who could help them along. Nearly everybody at Miss Smillie's was from somewhere else."

"Well, it's pretty late to think about that now," grumbled Lapham.

"And we've always gone our own way, and not looked out for the future. We ought to have gone out more, and had people come to the house. Nobody comes."

"Well, is that my fault? I guess nobody ever makes people welcomer."

"We ought to have invited company more."

"Why don't you do it now? If it's for the girls, I don't care if you have the house full all the while."

Mrs. Lapham was forced to a confession full of humiliation. "I don't know who to ask."

"Well, you can't expect me to tell you."

"No; we're both country people, and we've kept our

country ways; and we don't either of us, know what to do. You've had to work so hard, and your luck was so long coming, and then it came with such a rush, that we haven't had any chance to learn what to do with it. It's just the same with Irene's looks; I didn't expect she was ever going to have any, she *was* such a plain child, and, all at once, she's blazed out this way. As long as it was Pen that didn't seem to care for society, I didn't give much mind to it. But I can see it's going to be different with Irene. I don't believe but what we're in the wrong neighborhood."

"Well," said the Colonel, "there aint a prettier lot on the Back Bay than mine. It's on the water side of Beacon, and it's twenty-eight feet wide and a hundred and fifty deep. Let's build on it."

Mrs. Lapham was silent awhile. "No," she said finally; "we've always got along well enough here, and I guess we better stay."[69]

The dialogue, continuing without a major break from evening to morning, is beautifully structured. Husband and wife repeat one another's words offering slightly different interpretations of them. Persis uses *light* to mean "way of life" or "understanding" and Silas takes it up perhaps a bit sarcastically with an implication of "insight" as in "shedding new light." Persis takes his question in stride by downplaying her thoughts as "insight." She has simply accumulated certain facts for inspection, but she will not be deterred from explaining them. They infer from comments more than is actually said. Silas concludes that if Persis is interested in his Back Bay lot she might like a house there.

They assume conversational roles paralleling their personalities and roles in the marriage. Silas is a man of action; he looks for quick, dramatic solutions to problems. Persis is cautious, thoughtful, honestly naïve in social matters. Silas is de-

69. Howells, *Silas Lapham*, pp. 29-31.

cisive. If they're in the wrong neighborhood, then they only need to build in Back Bay. If they need more company, they need only invite people in. It is clear at this stage that money solves Silas' problems while Persis is far more aware that money cannot buy social standing or skills in social climbing.

Throughout the conversation, the narrator offers descriptive comments that support the interplay. He underscores Silas' defensiveness and competitiveness with his comment that Silas felt "a pang at the thought that he could possibly have been outdone." When the narrator labels Mrs. Lapham's admission of social inadequacy a "confession," he emphasizes her "humiliation."

The narrator establishes a pattern of speech for each character. Both have simple ways of expressing themselves. Both use "I guess" frequently; they speak in short sentences or coordinated structures and their vocabulary is limited and homely. Mrs. Lapham "didn't give much mind" to society; Irene has "blazed out." Silas uses the clipped " 'em" and the colloquial "aint" and "pretty" as in "pretty late." His "want me to build on it" is the only incomplete sentence in the dialogue. He uses two emphatic *I*'s and five of his eleven utterances begin with "well" or "oh, well"—fillers that cushion his responses to Persis.

The contrast between the Laphams' conversations and those of Bromfield and Anna Corey reveals the social and intellectual differences that separate the couples. The Corey conversations are more complex. Even the appearance of their conversations on the page differs from the short, choppy interchanges of the Laphams. They talk around their subject, viewing it from several perspectives. Bromfield is witty: he teases, makes satiric pronouncements, and plays with words. Anna counters with gravity and indulgence. She remonstrates, explains, and generally tries to exert some control over her life through control of Bromfield. In their first conversation of the novel, they discuss Tom's plan to go to work for Lapham.

"The girls were well," said Mrs. Corey, looking absently at her husband's brown velvet coat, in which he was so handsome . . .

"I am glad of that. The boy I have with me," he returned; "that is, when he *is* with me."

"Why, where is he?" demanded the mother.

"Probably carousing with the boon Lapham somewhere. He left me yesterday afternoon to go and offer his allegiance to the Mineral Paint King, and I haven't seen him since."

"Bromfield!" cried Mrs. Corey. "Why didn't you stop him?"

"Well, my dear, I'm not sure that it isn't a very good thing."

"A good thing? It's horrid!"

"No, I don't think so. It's decent. Tom had found out—without consulting the landscape, which I believe proclaims it everywhere—"

"Hideous!"

"That it's really a good thing; and he thinks that he has some ideas in regard to its dissemination in the parts beyond seas."

"Why shouldn't he go into something else?" lamented the mother.

"I believe he has gone into nearly everything else and come out of it. So there is a chance of his coming out of this. But as I had nothing to suggest in place of it, I thought it best not to interfere. In fact, what good would my telling him that mineral paint was nasty have done? I dare say *you* told him it was nasty."

"Yes! I did."

"And you see with what effect, though he values your opinion three times as much as he values mine. Perhaps you came up to tell him again that it was nasty?"

"I feel very unhappy about it. He is throwing himself away. Yes, I should like to prevent it if I could!"

The father shook his head.

"If Lapham hasn't prevented it, I fancy it's too late. But there may be some hopes of Lapham. As for Tom's throw-

ing himself away, I don't know. There's no question but he
is one of the best fellows under the sun. He's tremendously
energetic, and he has plenty of the kind of sense which we
call horse; but he isn't brilliant. No, Tom is not brilliant. I
don't think he would get on in a profession, and he's in-
stinctively kept out of everything of the kind. But he has
got to do something. What shall he do? He says mineral
paint, and really I don't see why he shouldn't. If money is
fairly and honestly earned, why should we pretend to care
what it comes out of, when we don't really care? That su-
perstition is exploded everywhere."

"Oh, it isn't the paint alone," said Mrs. Corey; and then
she perceptibly arrested herself, and made a diversion in
continuing: "I wish he had married some one."

"With money?" suggested her husband. "From time to
time I have attempted Tom's corruption from that side,
but I suspect Tom has a conscience against it, and I rather
like him for it. I married for love myself," said Corey,
looking across the table at his wife.

She returned his look tolerantly, though she felt it right
to say, "What nonsense!"

"Besides," continued her husband, "if you come to
money, there is the paint princess. She will have plenty."

"Ah, that's the worst of it," sighed the mother. "I suppose I could get on with the paint—"

"But not with the princess? I thought you said she was
a very pretty, well-behaved girl?"

"She is very pretty, and she is well-behaved; but there
is nothing of her. She is insipid; she is very insipid."

"But Tom seemed to like her flavor, such as it was?"

"How can I tell? We were under a terrible obligation
to them, and I naturally wished him to be polite to them.
In fact, I asked him to be so."

"And he was too polite?"

"I can't say that he was. But there is no doubt that the
child is extremely pretty."

"Tom says there are two of them. Perhaps they will
neutralize each other."

"Yes, there is another daughter," assented Mrs. Corey.

"I don't see how you can joke about such things, Bromfield," she added.

"Well, I don't either, my dear, to tell you the truth. My
hardihood surprises me. Here is a son of mine whom I
see reduced to making his living by a shrinkage in values.
It's very odd," interjected Corey, "that some values
should have this peculiarity of shrinking. You never hear
of values in a picture shrinking; but rents, stocks, real es-
tate—all those values shrink abominably. Perhaps it might
be argued that one should put all his values into pictures;
I've got a good many of mine there."

"Tom needn't earn his living," said Mrs. Corey, refusing her husband's jest. "There's still enough for all of us."

"That is what I have sometimes urged upon Tom. I
have proved to him that with economy, and strict attention to business, he need do nothing as long as he lives.
Of course he would be somewhat restricted, and it
would cramp the rest of us; but it is a world of sacrifices
and compromises. He couldn't agree with me, and he
was not in the least moved by the example of persons of
quality in Europe, which I alleged in support of the life
of idleness. It appears that he wishes to do something—to do something for himself. I am afraid that
Tom is selfish."[70]

Corey fancifully portrays Silas as a mock-heroic figure, "the
boon Lapham," with whom Tom is casting his lot. Mrs. Corey
is aghast at Tom's plan and upbraids her husband for his tol-
erance and amused attitude. Bromfield is more realistic about
Tom's expectations and explains both the boy's virtues and
his shortcomings in a lengthy speech characteristic of his role
in their exchanges. His later digressions on values and the
possibility of genteel poverty for Tom involve complex sentences and a playful use of words. He follows his train of
thought whimsically, away from the "serious" matter at hand.
Corey's speech seems somewhat contrived—full of well-

70. Ibid., pp. 93–96.

placed rhetorical questions and philosophical pronouncements on life—too polished and arranged, as Bridgman might
say—but it is very entertaining for the reader.

Anna is frequently evasive, or at least circumspect. She tries
to keep her baser thoughts from Bromfield, but he senses that
it is the social not the business commitment of Tom's new
job that worries her most. He finishes her vague "I wish he
had married some one" with an insightful comment, "with
money?" Since the narrator presents Anna's statement as
complete, it is never quite clear whether Corey is actually fin-
ishing her thought and speaking for her as well as himself.
He playfully espouses his theory of the wealthy daughter-in-
law and Anna tolerates his half-humorous discourse but is not
distracted from the main issue. She is preoccupied with "the
paint princess," as Bromfield labels Irene, and he wittily finishes her concession "I suppose I could get on with the
paint"—"But not with the princess." Corey waits for her to
provide him with information from the real world and then
he makes reality tolerable for them both by teasing it away.
They deal not so much with facts, as do the Laphams, but with
impressions.

The narrator often uses dramatic dialogues to reveal characters' personality traits that have not been evident elsewhere
in the novel. When Penelope tells her mother of Tom's love
for her and the mistake they have made about his interest in
Irene, her words capture a reserve of hostility and hurt as well
as her frustration. Mrs. Lapham's responses are appropriate
to her character—honest, even if they unwittingly perpetuate
the hurt to Penelope, and humble, taking responsibility for
the misunderstanding.

>   "Do you think," she [Mrs. Lapham] asked, simply, "that
> he got the idea you cared for him?"
>   "He knew it! How could I keep it from him? I said I
> didn't—at first!"
>   "It was no use," sighed the mother. "You might as well

said you did. It couldn't help Irene any, if you didn't."

"I always tried to help her with him, even when I—"

"Yes, I know. But she never was equal to him. I saw that from the start; but I tried to blind myself to it. And when he kept coming—"

"You never thought of me!" cried the girl, with a bitterness that reached her mother's heart. "I was nobody! I couldn't feel! No one could care for me!" The turmoil of despair, of triumph, of remorse and resentment, which filled her soul, tried to express itself in the words.

"No," said the mother humbly. "I didn't think of you. Or I didn't think of you enough. It did come across me sometimes that maybe—But it didn't seem as if—And your going on so for Irene—"

"You let me go on. You made me always go and talk with him for her, and you didn't think I would talk to him for myself. Well, I didn't!"

"I'm punished for it. When did you—begin to care for him?"

"How do I know? What difference does it make? It's all over now, no matter when it began. He won't come here any more, unless I let him." She could not help betraying her pride in this authority of hers, but she went on anxiously enough: "What will you say to Irene? She's safe as far as I'm concerned; but if he don't care for her, what will you do?"

"I don't know what to do," said Mrs. Lapham. She sat in an apathy from which she apparently could not rouse herself. "I don't see as anything can be done."

Penelope laughed in a pitying derision.[71]

Penelope's speech, her "droll medium" as Tom calls it,[72] is ordinarily wry and laconic. She often hides behind it, as in her exchanges with Mrs. Corey when that lady pays the Laphams a social call:

71. Ibid., pp. 226–27.
72. Ibid., p. 100.

> She [Mrs. Corey] looked at the girl searchingly again, as
> if to determine whether this were a touch of the drolling
> her son had spoken of. But she only added: "You will
> enjoy the sunsets on the Back Bay so much."
>
> "Well, not unless they're new ones," said Penelope. "I
> don't believe I could promise to enjoy any sunsets that
> I was used to, a great deal."
>
> Mrs. Corey looked at her with misgiving, hardening
> into dislike.[73]

Tom finds this refusal to play the conventional social games
refreshing; Mrs. Corey indulges such verbal play only in her
husband. Because of Penelope's usual detached good-humor,
her outburst of raw, personal emotion to her mother is more
powerful. In fact, she is on the verge of revealing even
more about herself and her growing attachment to Tom, "I
always tried to help her with him, even when I—," but her
mother interrupts her to discuss Irene. Words confound Mrs.
Lapham. She has no sense of verbal play, and she says what
she thinks. Her moral and social naïveté are reflected in her
language. She cares deeply for her family but their needs out-
strip her resources. She fails to comfort Penelope, and she
presents the facts to Irene with devastating severity.

> "Irene!" she said harshly, "there is something you have
> got to bear. It's a mistake we've all made. He don't care
> anything for you. He never did. He told Pen so last night.
> He cares for her."
>
> The sentences had fallen like blows. But the girl had
> taken them without flinching. She stood up immovable,
> but the delicate rose-light of her complexion went out
> and left her snow-white. She did not offer to speak.[74]

Irene's response to the crisis is to act not speak. She gathers
her keepsakes of Corey to dump on Penelope—a silent, but

73. Ibid., p. 166.
74. Ibid., p. 244.

dramatic display of anger and resignation. Subsequently, she buries herself in housework. She is practical—"sensible" Tom calls her—but inarticulate.

One of the most dramatic and significant conversations in the novel takes place between Tom Corey and Lapham after the fateful dinner party. The conversation reveals some of the narrator's ambivalence about Lapham and presents both positive and negative qualities in Corey, while brilliantly juxtaposing their worlds. The narrator opens the conversation at the end of the dinner party chapter (14): "Then he [Lapham] turned to the young man and demanded: "Was I drunk last night?' "[75] A dramatic pause, signalled by a chapter break, follows, and the scene reopens with a description of the physical confrontation between Lapham and Corey—a fine example of effective nonverbal communication in the novel.

> Lapham's strenuous face was broken up with the emotions that had forced him to this question: shame, fear of the things that must have been thought of him, mixed with a faint hope that he might be mistaken, which died out at the shocked and pitying look in Corey's eyes.
>
> "Was I drunk?" he repeated. "I ask you, because I was never touched by drink in my life before, and I don't know." He stood with his huge hands trembling on the back of his chair, and his dry lips apart, as he stared at Corey.
>
> "That is what every one understood, Colonel Lapham," said the young man. "Every one saw how it was. Don't—"
>
> "Did they talk it over after I left?" asked Lapham, vulgarly.
>
> "Excuse me," said Corey, blushing, "my father doesn't talk his guests over with one another." He added, with youthful superfluity, "You were among gentlemen."
>
> "I was the only one that wasn't a gentleman there!" lamented Lapham. "I disgraced you! I disgraced my family!

75. Ibid., p. 208.

I mortified your father before his friends!" His head dropped. "I showed that I wasn't fit to go with you. I'm not fit for any decent place. What did I say? What did I do?" he asked, suddenly lifting his head and confronting Corey. "Out with it! If you could bear to see it and hear it, I had ought to bear to know it!"

"There was nothing—really nothing," said Corey. "Beyond the fact that you were not quite yourself, there was nothing whatever. My father *did* speak of it to me," he confessed, "when we were alone. He said that he was afraid we had not been thoughtful of you, if you were in the habit of taking only water; I told him I had not seen wine at your table. The others said nothing about you."

"Ah, but what did they think?"

"Probably what we did: that it was purely a misfortune—an accident."

"I wasn't fit to be there," persisted Lapham. "Do you want to leave?" he asked, with savage abruptness.

"Leave?" faltered the young man.

"Yes; quit the business? Cut the whole connection?"

"I haven't the remotest idea of it!" cried Corey in amazement. "Why in the world should I?"

"Because you're a gentleman, and I'm not, and it ain't right I should be over you. If you want to go, I know some parties that would be glad to get you. I will give you up if you want to go before anything worse happens, and I sha'n't blame you. I can help you to something better than I can offer you here, and I will."

"There's no question of my going, unless you wish it," said Corey. "If you do—"

"Will you tell your father," interrupted Lapham, "that I had a notion all the time that I was acting the drunken blackguard, and that I've suffered for it all day? Will you tell him I don't want him to notice me if we ever meet, and that I know I'm not fit to associate with gentlemen in anything but a business way, if I am that?"

"Certainly I shall do nothing of the kind," retorted Corey. "I can't listen to you any longer. What you say is shocking to me—shocking in a way you can't think."

"Why, man!" exclaimed Lapham, with astonishment; "if *I* can stand it, *you* can!"

"No," said Corey, with a sick look, "that doesn't follow. You may denounce yourself, if you will; but I have my reasons for refusing to hear you—my reasons why I *can't* hear you. If you say another word I must go away."

"*I* don't understand you," faltered Lapham, in bewilderment, which absorbed even his shame.

"You exaggerate the effect of what has happened," said the young man. "It's enough, more than enough, for you to have mentioned the matter to me, and I think it's unbecoming in me to hear you."

He made a movement toward the door, but Lapham stopped him with the tragic humility of his appeal. "Don't go yet! I can't let you. I've disgusted you,—I see that; but I didn't mean to. I—I take it back."

"Oh, there's nothing to take back," said Corey, with a repressed shudder for the abasement which he had seen. "But let us say no more about it—think no more. There wasn't one of the gentlemen present last night who didn't understand the matter precisely as my father and I did, and that fact must end it between us two."[76]

Lapham's questions are blunt and his assertions powerful in their simplicity and humility. He cuts through Corey's gentlemanly evasions and lays bare his personal distress. Even in his humiliation he is generous. He offers Corey recommendations, should he want to leave. Howells clearly intends this interchange to reflect well on Silas. Silas' speech shows no signs of dialect, except for an "ain't." His hands tremble and he stutters in "the tragic humility of his appeal." At the same time, the narrator registers some of Corey's shock in his labels on Lapham's speech. Lapham speaks "vulgarly" and he asks his question about Tom's future "with savage abruptness." Howells seems to be telling the reader through his narrator that noble as Lapham's gesture is, it is not the act of a gentle-

76. Ibid., pp. 209–11.

man. He is, therefore, both moved and repelled by his character.[77]

Corey truly acts the gentleman in this scene. He holds Lapham at arm's length, unwilling to meet him on his terms. He invokes the conventions of polite society in dealing with a personally distasteful situation. His comment, " 'You were among gentlemen,' " is somewhat condescending and defensive. Rather than dismissing Lapham's plea to take a message to his father as unnecessary, Corey withdraws and expresses his repulsion: " 'What you say is shocking to me—shocking in a way you can't think.' " His final address to Lapham is uttered "with a repressed shudder at the abasement which he had seen." Although we learn later that Corey is distressed by Lapham's behavior because he wants to marry Lapham's daughter, he does, in fact, respond in a rather reserved manner to Lapham's anguish.

Howells' well-structured directly reported discourse is a key element in characterization and plot development, and it accounts for a very large proportion of the novel. His characters are always talking. Even the somewhat inarticulate Laphams talk a great deal, although their talk is not as fluent as the Coreys'. These characters represent a calculated range of talkers. At one extreme is Irene, who epitomizes the taciturn Lapham family. Her social aspirations, like her father's, are dashed, and she rehabilitates herself with hard work. Be-

77. Howells' ambivalent reaction to Lapham perhaps recalls his feelings about Twain's disrespectful speech at the famous Whittier dinner in December, 1877. Immediately after the dinner, Twain, filled with remorse, offered his apologies to the "gray Eminences," Longfellow, Emerson, and Whittier, whom he had made the brunt of his humorous storytelling. He was, however, ambivalent about the occasion in later years. Howells, who had invited Twain to speak, "was clearly frightened by the speech, not only for what it might do to Twain's good standing in Boston, but for what it might do to his own" (Kenneth Lynn, *William Dean Howells: An American Life*, [New York: Harcourt Brace Jovanovich, Inc., 1971], p. 177). Yet, Twain's humor may have, as Lynn suggests, "thrilled" Howells, for he had been made to feel an inferior interloper by Boston literary society (p. 177). Vanderbilt notes "the strong parallels between the Whittier and Corey dinners. . . ." *Achievement of Howells*, (pp. 135–36, fn. 54).

cause of her inarticulateness, the reader views her sympathetically but from a distance. At the other extreme is Bromfield Corey who discourses at great length on a wide range of subjects. His language, witty and entertaining, is a defense against reality. In between are the characters whose language reveals their struggles, who work to articulate their dilemmas. The narrator offers his interpretations discreetly, allowing the discourse to confront us continuously with the characters themselves.

indirectly reported discourse

Because directly reported discourse is clearly the dominant method of character presentation, Howells' indirectly reported discourse seems insignificant and less motivated by comparison. Howells' work, in general, has been criticized for his apparent shortcomings in reporting speech and thought indirectly. Carrington comments on Howells' "ignorance of the now-commonplace methods for getting at half-conscious or preconscious feelings and thoughts" and subjects Howells to the unfavorable comparison "even a self-taught author like Melville was able to master the principles of *erlebte Rede.* . . ."[78] Gordon O. Taylor in studying Howells' thought representation concludes: "Howells tends . . . to cast key observations about the nature of his characters' interior processes in the form of implied generalizations which avoid representing those processes 'in the particular connexion.' "[79] Such criticism underestimates Howells' technical skill because this skill is not employed consistently for the ends that interest the critics, that is, the representation of consciousness. Howells' view of his characters is largely an exte-

78. Carrington, *Immense Complex Drama,* pp. 190 and 191.

79. Gordon O. Taylor, *The Passages of Thought: Psychological Representation in the American Novel 1870–1900* (New York: Oxford University Press, 1969), p. 106.

rior one; therefore, his indirectly reported discourse—and *Silas Lapham* demonstrates a full range from diffused to compact—is neither as prominent nor as ambiguous as James's. Moreover, Howells uses ID largely to present characters' immediate reactions to scenes and events rather than to record complex, abstract thoughts. In this way, ID tends to heighten the drama rather than deepen the characterization.

Howells' most skillfully constructed ID serves the traditional narrative purpose of compacting DD. Thus, for example, the narrator sketches the conversation the Corey women have about a dinner party for the Laphams. He catches their tone without recording the conversation directly. The discussion begins with tagged compact ID, winds down to narrator summary that leads into an extensive and largely irrelevant narrator comment on Boston cousinships (the comment is not quoted here):

> They said, What harm could giving the dinner possibly do them? They might ask any or all of their acquaintance without disadvantage to themselves; but it would be perfectly easy to give the dinner just the character they chose, and still flatter the ignorance of the Laphams. The trouble would be with Tom, if he were really interested in the girl; but he could not say anything if they made it a family dinner; he could not feel anything. They had each turned in her own mind, as it appeared from a comparison of ideas, to one of the most comprehensive of those cousinships which form the admiration and terror of the adventurer in Boston society.[80]

All of the Corey women think alike on this subject, so it is not necessary to quote them individually. This report foreshadows some neatly compressed discussions Silas has with other businessmen at the climax of the novel.

Silas Lapham himself is involved in the majority of the novel's indirectly reported discourse. These reports, which

80. Howells, *Silas Lapham*, p. 172.

center on two events, the Corey-Lapham dinner party and Lapham's rapid and inexorable business decline, are remarkably different in purpose and form. Lapham at the dinner party is an outsider, an observer, but his observations are naïve and mistaken, ultimately colored by intoxication, both physical and emotional. The reader is doubly removed from Lapham in the scene, for the reader witnesses both the obvious evidence of Lapham's humiliation and Lapham's own misperceptions about it. In the extended reports of his business dealings and his thoughts about them, the narrator presents Lapham more sympathetically without the ironic distance of the dinner party sequence. His thoughts reveal his business acumen and the depths of his problems; they also reveal his pride and tenacity.

From the Laphams' arrival at the Coreys' for dinner we weave in and out of Silas' point of view, marked by his word choice and reflecting his perceptions. For example, the narrator describes the pre-dinner ritual and slips briefly into Silas' thoughts and then out again.

> Lapham had never seen people go down to dinner arm-in-arm before, but he knew that his wife was distinguished in being taken out by the host, and he waited in jealous impatience to see if Tom Corey would offer his arm to Irene. He gave it to that big girl they called Miss Kingsbury, and the handsome old fellow whom Mrs. Corey had introduced as her cousin took Irene out.[81]

Only the phrases "that big girl they called Miss Kingsbury" and "the handsome old fellow" are directly attributable to Lapham. At dinner, when Lapham overhears Tom Corey and Irene talking about Penelope, the narrator tells us: "It vexed him to think she had not come; she could have talked as well as any of them; she was just as bright; and Lapham was aware that Irene was not as bright. . . ."[82] The middle two clauses

81. Ibid., p. 190.
82. Ibid., p. 196.

clearly represent Lapham's thoughts, framed by narrator-introduced clauses. The narrator does not necessarily share Lapham's evaluation of Penelope.

After dinner as Lapham becomes increasingly inebriated, he loses his inhibitions, and the narrator presents the scene where he disgraces himself largely from his perspective.

> He lost the reserve which he had maintained earlier, and began to boast . . . As he cast off all fear, his voice rose, and he hammered his arm-chair with the thick of his hand for emphasis. Mr. Corey seemed impressed; he sat perfectly quiet, listening, and Lapham saw the other gentlemen stop in their talk every now and then to listen. After this proof of his ability to interest them, he would have liked to have Mrs. Lapham suggest again that he was unequal to their society, or to the society of anybody else . . . He did not understand why young Corey seemed so preoccupied, and he took occasion to tell the company how he had said to his wife the first time he saw that fellow that he could make a man of him if he had him in the business; and he guessed he was not mistaken. He began to tell stories of the different young men he had had in his employ. At last he had the talk altogether to himself; no one else talked, and he talked unceasingly. It was a great time; it was a triumph.[83]

Many of the impressions recorded here are not necessarily rendered as Lapham's thoughts. The narrator tells us what Lapham saw—"he [Mr. Corey] sat perfectly still . . ."—and offers Lapham's conclusion that Corey "seemed impressed." The reader and narrator know otherwise, just as they understand "why young Corey seemed so preoccupied." The ironic tension of this presentation makes Lapham's predicament seem all the more excruciating. In fact, two layers of indirection are involved in Lapham's comment on Tom Corey—"he could make a man of him if he had him in the business." The

83. Ibid., p. 205.

narrator quotes Lapham indirectly and Lapham quotes himself. The last two sentences of this paragraph are the most interesting. The sentence beginning "at last" registers both the narrator's and Lapham's observation, but the "at last" is clearly Lapham's thought. He has been waiting for an opportunity to shine and in the last sentence of compact ID, so contrary to fact, he believes that he has succeeded.

As Lapham takes leave of the party, the narrator records his speech indirectly, but a direct address form slips into the representation.

NARRATOR/ LAPHAM	Ten years ago he, Silas Lapham, had come to Boston, a little worse off than nothing at all, for he was in debt for half the money that he had bought out his partner with,
LAPHAM	and here he was now worth a million, and meeting you gentlemen like one of you. And every cent of that was honest money,—no speculation,—every copper of it for value received. And here, only the other day, his old part-
NARRATOR/ LAPHAM	ner, who had been going to the dogs ever since he went out of the business, came and borrowed twenty thousand dollars of him! Lapham lent it because his wife wanted him to: she had always felt bad about the fellow's having to go out of the business.[84]

Classically free indirect, the speech is as close to direct discourse as ID can be. The narrator retains Silas' personal references ("he, Silas Lapham"), the direct address ("you gentlemen"), the exclamation, the deictic markers ("here," "now"), and the vocabulary ("a little worse off than nothing at all," "going to the dogs"). Narrator control is evident in the third-person pronouns and past-tense verbs of the first and last two sentences, but the emphatic fragment in the middle—"and every cent of that was honest money"—moves entirely into Lapham's voice. This pattern resembles Huck's record of the King's "Tears and Flapdoodle" speech dis-

84. Ibid., p. 296.

cussed in the next chapter. The difference between this presentation and Huck's involves the narrator's attitude. Unlike Huck, the narrator does not openly express his contempt for Lapham's boasting. He remains aloof, allowing the reader to draw his own conclusion. But by presenting it as free indirect discourse, the narrator is more involved than he would be in DD, and the presentation is, paradoxically, more personal and affecting.[85]

This scene climaxes one part of the novel. It demonstrates the futility of Silas' social aspirations; he does not belong in the Back Bay world. He humbles himself to Tom Corey in his apology, but, interestingly, the narrator leaves it to Tom to offer the last word on Lapham's behavior, and Tom's conclusions constitute one of the few passages in the novel approximating interior monologue.

> He thought of him [Lapham] the night before in the company of those ladies and gentlemen, and he quivered in resentment of his vulgar, braggart, uncouth nature. He recognized his own allegiance to the exclusiveness to which he was born and bred . . . His eyes fell on the porter going about in his shirt-sleeves to make the place fast for the night, and he said to himself that Dennis was not more plebeian than his master; that the gross appetites, the blunt sense, the purblind ambition, the stupid arrogance were the same in both, and the difference was in a brute will that probably left the porter the gentler man of the two . . . Amidst the stings and flashes of his wounded pride, all the social traditions, all the habits of feeling, which he had silenced more and more by force of will during the past months, asserted their natural sway, and he rioted in his contempt of the offensive boor, who was even more offensive in his shame than in his trespass. He said

85. Throughout the novel, the reader never really knows the circumstances surrounding Lapham's buying out Rogers. Mrs. Lapham thinks he forced Rogers out; Silas is uneasy about the transaction but defends it as necessary for business. Here the narrator offers a scrupulously neutral description of the event, "the fellow's having to go out of the business," which reflects Silas' perspective without judging it.

to himself that he was a Corey, as if that were somewhat; yet he knew that at the bottom of his heart all the time was that which must control him at last . . . It was almost with the girl's voice that it seemed to plead with him, to undo in him, effect by effect, the work of his indignant resentment, to set all things in another and fairer light, to give him hopes, to suggest palliations, to protest against injustices. It *was* in Lapham's favor that he was so guiltless in the past, and now Corey asked himself if it were the first time he could have wished a guest at his father's table to have taken less wine; whether Lapham was not rather to be honored for not knowing how to contain his folly where a veteran transgressor might have held his tongue. He asked himself, with a thrill of sudden remorse, whether, when Lapham humbled himself in the dust so shockingly, he had shown him the sympathy to which such *abandon* had the right; and he had to own that he had met him on the gentlemanly ground, sparing himself and asserting the superiority of his sort, and not recognizing that Lapham's humiliation came from the sense of wrong, which he had helped to accumulate upon him by superfinely standing aloof and refusing to touch him.[86]

Lapham's "vulgar, braggart, uncouth nature" is the narrator's description, but the most brutal judgments of this passage are largely attributable to Corey. Although the comparison of Lapham to Dennis is presented indirectly, the narrator specifically labels it as Corey's. Responsibility for the reference to Lapham as an "offensive boor," however, is ambiguous. The narrator describes Tom's pride and although the use of *the* before "offensive boor" sounds as if it were Tom's thought, the narrator may be responsible for the label. In the following sentence, it is unclear whether the cynical disclaimer "as if that were somewhat" about his own background is Corey's or the narrator's. The narrator describes the effects of Corey's memory of Penelope (Penelope is Tom's conscience

86. Howells, *Silas Lapham*, pp. 211–12.

here), but Tom's change of heart is rendered in what seem to be his own words. The emphases *(was, abandon)* are direct discourse forms, and although the reasoning is a little complex for spontaneous thought, it would appear that Howells wishes the reader to take these ideas as Corey's. Nowhere does Tom demonstrate so clearly his role as "a link between the old order and the new."[87] He simultaneously despises and sympathizes with Lapham.

At the conclusion of the novel, the narrator compresses a series of Silas' business negotiations in indirectly reported discourse; the style intensifies the rapidity of Silas' descent. The fact that these key events take the form of "speech events," that is, conversations involving Silas' alternatives and decisions, reflects once again Howells' commitment to "objective" drama. The narrator makes the reader privy to the transactions rather than summarizing them. The intense negotiations Lapham undertakes with a West Virginia firm to salvage the market for his paint appear first as an indirect summary of Lapham's pitch, then, after a pause for lunch, a summary of the partners' response. By compressing the discussions in this way, the narrator is able to sketch in some telling details about the West Virginians and, by comparison, about Lapham.

> He admitted that they had a good thing, and that he should have to fight them hard; but he meant to fight them to the death unless they could come to some sort of terms. Now, the question was whether they had better go on and make a heavy loss for both sides by competition, or whether they had better form a partnership . . . Let them name a figure at which they would buy, a figure at which they would sell . . .
> They talked all day, going out to lunch together at the Astor House, and sitting with their knees against the

87. "Realism Defined: William Dean Howells," *Literary History of the United States: History*, ed. R. E. Spiller, *et. al.*, 4th ed., rev. (New York: Macmillan, 1974), p. 892.

> counter on a row of stools before it for fifteen minutes
> of reflection and deglutition, with their hats on . . . At
> last, they said what they would do. They said it was non-
> sense to talk of buying Lapham out, for they had not the
> money. . . .[88]

Howells cannot resist satirizing these provincials involved in
"reflection and deglutition, with their hats on." His picture
is a wonderfully insightful view of both the simplicity and the
intensity of Lapham's business world.

During this stressful time Lapham alternately offers himself
encouragement, often in the form of bravado, and strong
doses of reality. When he arrives home from his negotiations
with the West Virginians, he contemplates the prospects of
raising the capital they want from him.

> He could raise fifteen thousand on his Nankeen Square
> house, and another fifteen on his Beacon Street lot, and
> this was all that a man who was worth a million by rights
> could do! He said a million, and he said it in defiance of
> Bellingham, who had subjected his figures to an analysis
> which wounded Lapham more than he chose to show at
> the time, for it proved that he was not so rich and not so
> wise as he had seemed. His hurt vanity forbade him to go
> to Bellingham now for help or advice. . . .[89]

The passage is an interesting blend of compact ID and narrator comment. The opening sentence with its exclamatory conclusion seems to be entirely Lapham's thought. The comment
on his claim to millionaire status combines the narrator's and
Lapham's voices. The emphasis—"He said a million, and he
said it in defiance . . ."—seems to be Lapham to himself, but
the narrator offers the explanation of his need to defy Bellingham.

The same combination of narrator explanation and almost

88. Howells, *Silas Lapham*, pp. 317–18.
89. Ibid., p. 319.

unfiltered character thought appears in Lapham's negotiations with Rogers and Rogers' shady English clients. The narrator describes Lapham's sense of the situation with a comment on the lack of realism in art.

> He had expected to come into that room and unmask Rogers, and have it over. But he had unmasked Rogers without any effect whatever, and the play had only begun. He had a whimsical and sarcastic sense of its being very different from the plays at the theater. He could not get up and go away in silent contempt. . . .[90]

When Lapham leaves this encounter, the narrator describes his struggle to decide the matter.

> He walked out into the night air, every pulse throbbing with the strong temptation. He knew very well those men would wait, and gladly wait, till the morning, and that the whole affair was in his hands. It made him groan in spirit to think that it was. If he had hoped that some chance might take the decision from him, there was no such chance, in the present or future, that he could see. It was for him alone to commit this rascality—if it was a rascality—or not.[91]

Again the narrator's voice combines with Lapham's. The emphasis, "knew very well," "and gladly wait," and the confusion, "if it was a rascality," reflect Lapham's perspective, if not his exact words, and they are surrounded by the narrator's sympathetic descriptions of his plight.

These lengthy explorations of his problems immediately precede Lapham's final confrontation with Rogers in Persis' presence. After a directly reported conversation with Rogers, Lapham struggles with his conscience through the night, as Persis listens to his pacing. The terms of his struggle are not recorded. Taylor notes: "He [Howells] also leaves the crucial

90. Ibid., p. 325.
91. Ibid., p. 326.

phase of Lapham's interior process—a nightlong vigil of searching self-analysis which, like Isabel Archer's, is intended by the novelist to enable the character to 'see' with greater inward clarity—off the narrative stage altogether."[92] This night *is* the climax of Silas' debate with himself about the questionable deal, but I doubt that Howells' intention parallels James's, for Lapham gains no insights from his vigil. The scene is not designed to tell the reader about Lapham or his perceptions but to demonstrate the enormity of his problems.

Taylor correctly identifies "Howells' disinterest in the unbroken 'view from within,' in the Jamesian sense."[93] Howells prefers the "view from without." Thus even in his quite extensive presentation of Lapham's thoughts, the narrator does not give us an "unbroken" view. He aids Lapham in the articulation of his problems, but this intermingling of narrator and character perspectives produces very little "Jamesian" ambiguity. The narrator shares his character's confusion, and the character comes to a sufficiently realistic view of himself to see his shortcomings. One passage in the novel, however, involves an interesting ambiguity. Lapham never actually makes the decision to reject the Englishmen; it is made for him when he receives an offer for the mills that precludes his selling them. Thus his moral victory rests on procrastination rather than decisive action. When he receives the offer, he shows it to Rogers, who lashes out at him:

> "You've ruined me!" Rogers broke out. "I haven't a cent left in the world! God help my poor wife!"
> He went out, and Lapham remained staring at the door which closed upon him. This was his reward for standing firm for right and justice to his own destruction: to feel like a thief and a murderer.[94]

92. Taylor, *Passages of Thought*, p. 100.
93. Ibid.
94. Howells, *Silas Lapham*, pp. 331–32.

The narrator describes Rogers' exit, but it is unclear whether
the narrator or Silas or both believe that he has been "standing firm for right and justice to his own destruction." Responsibility here is significant because it involves a judgment of
Silas. The sentence lacks an introductory tag, but the sentiment seems to be Silas'. The reader cannot really come to a
conclusion about the narrator's attitude.

Silas' business failure takes a peculiar toll on Persis. Having
been cut off from his business life and clinging tenaciously
to "her old remorse for that questionable act of his"[95] towards Rogers, she fails as an advisor and succumbs to a vi-
cious jealousy prompted in part by an anonymous note
(obviously from Rogers) about her husband's "lady copying-
clerk."[96] The narrator records her mental accusations against
Lapham at great length:

> A thousand things thronged into her mind to support her
> in her evil will. She remembered how glad and proud that
> man had been to marry her, and how everybody said she
> was marrying beneath her when she took him. She re-
> membered how good she had always been to him, how
> perfectly devoted, slaving early and late to advance him,
> and looking out for his interests in all things, and sparing
> herself in nothing. If it had not been for her, he might
> have been driving stage yet; and since their troubles had
> begun, the troubles which his own folly and imprudence
> had brought on them, her conduct had been that of a true
> and faithful wife. Was *he* the sort of man to be allowed
> to play her false with impunity?[97]

Her concerns seem petty when contrasted with Silas', and
she turns on him when he is at his lowest point. The narrator captures her irrational fury in what amounts to an interior monologue rendered as compact ID. The paratactic

95. Ibid., p. 329.
96. Ibid., p. 337.
97. Ibid., p. 338.

sentence constructions, the emphasis *(he)*, the question form, the vocabulary expressing her own views ("perfectly devoted," "slaving early and late," "his own folly and imprudence"), the references ("that man") all mark this passage as free indirect or compact ID. Howells deepens and complicates Persis' character to demonstrate the negative impact that Silas' financial rise has had on their lives. Thus this digression into Persis' consciousness, while it adds little to the plot, enhances both the characterization and the moral lesson of the novel.

As his voice mingles with those of his characters, the narrator of *Silas Lapham* becomes more intimately involved in their circumstances and erases some of the distance his "objectivity" creates. Yet within the indirectly reported discourse, the narrator continuously reserves the right to judge and interpret for his characters. He never completely relinquishes his control.

The narrator of *The Bostonians* develops a greater sympathy for his characters as the story evolves, but the extent to which he empathizes with them is difficult for the reader to ascertain. The resulting ambiguity seems largely unintentional. The narrator starts out by satirizing all of his characters but loses his detachment in telling the story and absorbing the characters' perspectives. The narrator of *Silas Lapham* maintains his detachment throughout the novel. Despite the rather lengthy records of Silas' and Persis' thoughts, the narrator does not shift to his characters' perspective or "center of knowing," and he deliberately obscures his own sympathies. The reader may choose to like or dislike Silas; the narrator merely presents the information he has gathered.

After Silas' business collapse becomes a certainty, the narrator ceases to give us Silas' perspective. He describes Silas as possessing "a sort of pensive dignity that refined his rudeness to an effect that sometimes comes to such natures after long sickness, when the animal strength has been taxed and lowered."[98] While the portrayal is sympathetic, it is coolly detached and implicitly condescending—"rudeness," "such natures," "animal strength." Several more passages describe Silas' humbled, but honorable state—"All those who were concerned in his affairs said he behaved well, and even more than well, when it came to the worst"; "He was more broken than he knew by his failure; it did not kill, . . . but it weakened the spring once so strong and elastic"[99]—but we know nothing of Silas' feelings. In fact, Silas becomes a type ("such natures") and his experience an excuse for the narrator to moralize: "Adversity had so far been his friend that it had taken from him all hope of the social success for which people crawl and truckle, and restored him, through failure and doubt and heartache, the manhood which his prosperity had so nearly stolen from him."[100]

Thus the narrator assesses and explains Silas' "rise," but Silas' experiences change him very little. At the end of the novel, Silas entertains the minister, Sewell, who reflects the narrator's detachment in that he "was intensely interested in the moral spectacle which Lapham presented under his changed conditions."[101] In answer to Sewell's question about regrets, the novel closes with Silas' own words: " 'I don't know as I should always say it paid; but if I done it, and the thing was to do over again, right in the same way, I guess I should have to do it.' "[102] The narrator discreetly refrains from commenting on this avowal, but the reader can see that it is appropriate to Silas' character. Silas' circumstances not his outlook have changed, and it would seem that his own aspirations and mistakes rather than the system do him in.

Ultimately, the narrator of *Silas Lapham* seems to deny control but not relinquish it. Had he simply allowed the charac-

98. Ibid., p. 349.
99. Ibid., pp. 352 and 354.
100. Ibid., p. 359.
101. Ibid., p. 363.
102. Ibid., p. 365.

ters to speak for themselves, he would have attained the objectivity he sought. But he breaks in with comments on characters and events that vitiate this objectivity; moreover, his heavy-handed demurrers, his signs of tentativeness, make the narrative technique too obvious. His need to control characterization without seeming to control it contributes to a sense that these characters are "small"; they remain types rather than growing into people. If Howells had finished the novel on the note of narrator/character harmony he achieves in the sequences recording Lapham's thoughts, the novel would have been a more interesting work of art, involving fuller characterization and an advance in the presentation of character.

Howells' presentation reflects the complications of the realistic technique he himself articulated. These complications put Howells at war with his own craft; he was caught in the paradox of his commitment to "truth." He chose the historical novel, the most traditional form, because despite the fact that "the form involves a thousand contradictions, improbabilities," in its finest manifestations ". . . nothing in fiction is more impressive, more convincing of its truth."[103] Having adopted this form, he attempted to pare away some of its imperfections; he tries to "content himself and his reader with conjecture as to his people's motives and with report of them from hearsay. . . ."[104] Nevertheless, his conjectures must give way to the "grotesque absurdity" involved when the historical novelist "enters into the minds and hearts of his characters. . . ."[105]

Moreover, the novelist must act as a guide, not simply a recorder of facts. He must, in Bromfield Corey's words, "interpret the common feelings of commonplace people. . . ."[106] In his essay "On Truth in Fiction," Howells comments:

103. Howells, "Novel-Writing and Novel-Reading," p. 23.
104. Ibid.
105. Ibid.
106. Howells, *Silas Lapham*, p. 202.

> When realism becomes false to itself, when it heaps up facts merely, and maps life, instead of picturing it, realism will perish too. Every true realist instinctively knows this, and it is perhaps the reason why he is careful of every fact, and feels himself bound to express or to indicate its meaning at the risk of over-moralizing.[107]

When Howells' narrator "over-moralizes" in order to avoid leaving merely a "map" of Silas' "rise," the reader is robbed of the right to interpretation.

A reader might find the disturbing ambiguity of *The Bostonians* more satisfying than the closed frame of *Silas Lapham*, but both James and Howells were troubled by the realistic narrator's right to control. For both novelists, the narrator's presence in the text undermines the illusion of life because it makes the novel a novel, and therefore potentially only "make believe," as James says. If, however, the narrator is a "historian," then he is dealing with truth, not fantasy. If, in addition, he admits his limitations, his humility convinces the reader of his honesty. The narrator/historian who shows his characters speaking and thinking for themselves additionally preserves the illusion; but in this rendering of discourse there is a fine line between telling and showing.

Howells felt best able to preserve the illusion with direct discourse; however, the appropriateness and vitality of his DD make it easy to overlook the significance of his indirect discourse. His technical advances with various forms of ID, for example, in the dinner party scene, rival James's. ID creates tension, adds ironic distance, compresses and focuses. In this novel it is largely unambiguous, reflecting little of the confusion between narrator and character perspective so typical of James. Nevertheless, ID tends to diminish the narrator's role. Both authors develop innovative means to present discourse of all types in order to highlight the autonomy of their charac-

107. William Dean Howells, "On Truth in Fiction," in *Documents of Modern Literary Realism*, ed. George J. Becker (Princeton: Princeton University Press, 1963), p. 136.

ters. But neither author is willing to relinquish the narrator's control; at best, the narrator becomes less a puppeteer and more an intermediary between reader and character. For Howells, the narrator is necessary to interpret facts into art. Twain, too, expands the forms and function of discourse and merges narrator and character in Huck Finn in order to achieve authorial control and detachment, yet he also has trouble closing the frame.

4

adventures
of
huckleberry
finn:
sophisticated
naïveté

Adventures of Huckleberry Finn is Mark Twain's[1] mas-
terpiece: a triumph in American literature. Representing a
successful and unique coalescence of setting, characterization
and style, the novel climaxed Twain's career. Thousands of
pages of critical commentary have analyzed and evaluated the
book. Although not as widely praised in Twain's lifetime as
some of his other works, it has always had its admirers and
champions, and it has gained stature throughout the twenti-
eth century, praised by such prominent writers as Eliot and
Hemingway as well as by countless critics. Although always
a little uneasy with a novel written so clearly for "the Belly

1. I refer to the author of *Adventures of Huckleberry Finn* as Mark Twain throughout
this study. The complex relationship between Samuel Clemens and his fanciful
pseudonym for his public persona is too complex to explore here (see, for example,
Justin Kaplan, *Mr. Clemens and Mark Twain: A Biography* [N.Y.: Simon and Schuster,
1966]). Some of Clemens' earlier works (*Roughing It,* for example), are narrated by
Mark Twain, and there is some ironic distance between Clemens, the author, and
Twain, the narrator. Huck tells the reader that he first appears in *The Adventures of
Tom Sawyer,* "made by Mr. Mark Twain." The reader is thus directed to take Clemens'
public personality as the "implied" author of *Huck Finn.*

and the Members," as Twain once described his work by contrast with literature for the "Head,"[2] Howells expressed his
appreciation in his definitive essay "Mark Twain: An Inquiry"
(1901): ". . . I who like *The Connecticut Yankee in King Arthur's
Court* so much have half a mind to give my whole heart to
Huckleberry Finn."[3]

The novel has been criticized largely in two areas. Its "dis-
reputable hero"[4] and "strong" language troubled contempo-
rary genteel reviewers and got it banned periodically from
local libraries.[5] More significant is the continuing debate over
the way Twain chose to end the story. By having Huck and
Tom Sawyer turn Jim's plight into a sham romance, Twain
has been accused of subverting the themes of the novel and
abandoning Huck's moral growth. There are many plausible
theories about Twain's motivations for the burlesque ending,
some damning and some justifying,[6] but the most interesting

2. "Letter to Andrew Lang 1890 (?)" in *Mark Twain: The Critical Heritage*, ed. Frederick Anderson (London: Routledge & Kegan Paul, 1971), p. 334.

3. William Dean Howells, *My Mark Twain: Reminiscences and Criticisms*, ed. with
intro. by Marilyn Austin Baldwin (Baton Rouge: Louisiana State University Press,
1967), p. 150. Howells gives this description of the novel: ". . . such a book as *Huckleberry Finn* takes itself out of the order of romance and places itself with the great
things in picaresque fiction. Still, it is more poetic than picaresque, and of a deeper
psychology . . . In the boy's history the author's fancy works realistically to an end
as high as it has reached elsewhere, if not higher . . ." (p. 150). Yet, although Howells
credits James with using the "autobiographical" novel form to create work "of really
unimpeachable perfection" ("Novel-Writing and Novel-Reading: An Impersonal Explanation," ed. William M. Gibson, in *Howells and James: A Double Billing* [New York:
The New York Public Library, 1958], p. 23), he fails to mention *Huck Finn* in the
"autobiographical" category.

4. Arthur L. Scott, "Introduction," *Mark Twain: Selected Criticism* (Dallas: Southern
Methodist University Press, 1955), p. 4.

5. See "Boston *Transcript* and Springfield *Republican* (Banned in Boston: The Con-
cord Public Library Uproar)," p. 285, in Samuel Langhorne Clemens, *Adventures of
Huckleberry Finn: An Authoritative Text, Backgrounds and Sources, Criticism*, ed. Sculley
Bradley, Richmond Croom Beatty, E. Hudson Long, Thomas Cooley (New York:
W. W. Norton & Company, Inc., 1977). All page references to the text itself will be
from this version of the first American edition.

6. See, for example, essays by Lionel Trilling, T. S. Eliot, Leo Marx, James Cox,
and Roy Harvey Pearce in the "Criticism" section of *Adventures of Huckleberry Finn*
(New York: W. W. Norton, 1977). Virtually every critic who writes on the novel has
a theory about the motivation for and the appropriateness of the ending.

explanations for this study center around the issue of authorial intrusion on the very autonomous narrator. Although
Huck continues to narrate the story, Twain gives him less control over both the events and the narration.

Huck Finn has many features in common with *The Bostonians*
and *The Rise of Silas Lapham.* It is written in the first person,
albeit of the personal rather than the rhetorical type; it is peo-
pled with characters drawn from a setting the author knew
intimately; its ending is flawed by a failure to follow through
with the natural evolution of its narrative strategy. In addition, despite the apparent limitations imposed by the "naïve"
narrator, the novel is rich in a wide range of discourse representation. The novel has been repeatedly praised for its many
virtues: its evocation of the quintessential American experience, its characterization, its morality, its originality. Over
and above all of these accomplishments stands the *Huck Finn*
style. In many ways, *Huck Finn* is a book about language.
Huck's language is his vision, and his vision is both profound
and unique.

Tony Tanner notes that "from the start of his writing career, Clemens reveals a preoccupation with language problems."[7] Twain was no match for Howells or James in literary
theorizing. Gibson is correct when he observes that ". . .
Clemens did not in his own day appear to be a 'man of letters'
in the sense that James and Howells and Eliot were men of
letters, and . . . he exercised his art less consciously than they
did, and with less interest in theory."[8] However, he was very
sophisticated about language use and structure. An accomplished platform speaker and storyteller, he valued spoken
language equally with written, while recognizing the difference between the two. To insure the authenticity of dialect
in written form, he went through the painstaking process of

7. Tony Tanner, *The Reign of Wonder: Naivety and Reality in American Literature* (New
York: Harper and Row, Perennial Library, 1967), p. 105.

8. William M. Gibson, *The Art of Mark Twain* (New York: Oxford University Press,
1976), p. 4.

"talking and talking and *talking* till it sounds right."[9] A more crucial interaction was involved in his evaluation of written works, his own and others, which he subjected to "the most exacting of tests—the reading aloud."[10] His respect for and understanding of the spoken word and its power of expression led him to try to capture some of its qualities in his written style and in his presentation of all types of discourse.

Four years after completing *Huck Finn,* Twain explored the complex relationship between spoken and written language in a note to an interviewer, Edward Bok:

> Spoken speech is one thing, written speech is quite another . . . The moment "talk" is put into print you recognize that it is not what it was when you heard it; you perceive that an immense something has disappeared from it. That is its very soul . . . To add interpretations [to talk] which would convey the right meaning is a something which would require—what? An art so high and fine and difficult that no possessor of it would ever be allowed to waste it on interviews.[11]

It is this art, this ability to maintain the semblance of talk in written form while at the same time investing it with the spirit and animation of the speaker, that informs and controls the narrative voice of *Huck Finn.*[12]

Twain's passionate commitment to the effective use of language was the basis of his realistic technique. Honest language is accurate and clear; it does not succumb to pretension or bombast. Summarizing his standards late in life he said:

9. Samuel Langhorne Clemens, *Mark Twain's Letters,* ed. Albert Bigelow Paine (New York: Harper & Brothers, 1917) I: 227.

10. Clemens, *Letters* II, p. 797.

11. Ibid., pp. 504–5.

12. This art is also a feature of Perry Miller's "plain style": "the fantastic requirement of the plain style, whether in the Puritan sermon or in *Huckleberry Finn,* is simply that language as printed on the page must convey the emphasis, the hesitancies, the searchings of language as it is spoken" (Perry Miller, *Nature's Nation* [Cambridge: Belknap Press of Harvard University Press, 1967], p. 232).

"I like the exact word, and clarity of statement, and here and there a touch of good grammar for picturesqueness. . . ."[13] In "My Methods of Writing" he concentrates on diction with his now classic statement: "the difference between the *almost* right and the *right* word is really a large matter—it's the difference between the lightning-bug and the lightning."[14] Thus one of his severest criticisms of another writer, Fenimore Cooper, was that his "word-sense was singularly dull."[15] He praises Howells because "he seems to be almost always able to find that elusive and shifty grain of gold, the *right word.*"[16] The right word for Twain had to meet two principal tests: it had to reflect accurately what the speaker/writer saw or heard, and it had to sound convincing in context.

Like Howells, Twain was a Westerner seeking a place in the Eastern literary establishment. Unlike Howells he was always ambivalent about that world and his allegiance to it. In his predictably contradictory way, he chose *Huck Finn* as his favorite work on one occasion, while selecting the vastly inferior, but more genteel *Personal Recollections of Joan of Arc* on another.[17] Although he could imitate acceptable modes of

13. Samuel Langhorne Clemens, *Mark Twain's Autobiography,* ed. Albert Bigelow Paine (New York: Harper & Brothers, 1924) I: 173.

14. Samuel Langhorne Clemens, "My Methods of Writing," *Mark Twain Quarterly* 8 (Winter-Spring 1949): 1.

15. Samuel Langhorne Clemens, "Fenimore Cooper's Literary Offenses," in *Literary Essays,* vol. 22 of *The Writings of Mark Twain,* Author's National Edition (New York: Harper & Brothers, 1918), p. 75.

16. Samuel Langhorne Clemens, "William Dean Howells" (1906) rpt. in *Howells: A Century of Criticism,* ed. Kenneth E. Eble (Dallas: Southern Methodist University Press, 1962), p. 79. It is interesting to compare Twain's pronouncements to those of Roman Jakobson "On Realism in Art" (1921): ". . . when we want our speech to be candid, natural, and expressive, we discard the usual polite etiquette and call things by their real names. They have a fresh ring, and we feel that they are 'the right words' " (*Readings in Russian Poetics: Formalist and Structuralist Views,* ed. Ladislav Matejka and Krystyna Pomorska [Ann Arbor, Michigan: Slavic Publications, 1978], p. 40).

17. Walter Blair quotes the following lines from an October 14, 1895, interview in *The South Australian Register:* "Now which of your own books do you like best?" "Well, I think 'Huckleberry Finn' " (*Mark Twain & Huck Finn* [Berkeley and Los Angeles: University of California Press, 1960], p. 371). Albert Bigelow Paine reprints

genteel writing, he attempted through his style in *Huck Finn* to give expression to what Henry Nash Smith calls the vernacular values of "homely wisdom and rugged honesty that were an implicit indictment of empty elegance and refinement."[18] Thus Twain turned a romantic belief in the power of language into a theory of realism. Style, the way in which an idea is expressed, is inextricably linked to the character of the observer. Style in language is a reflection of the speaker's personality and mode of perception.

Twain's naïve, unpretentious characters express themselves simply and often eloquently. They perceive events and scenes unself-consciously, unlike his more educated narrators and characters who often are prevented from an honest response by their preconceived expectations and knowledge. His writing prior to *Huck Finn* is most original when recording characters like Scotty Briggs in *Roughing It* (1872), Colonel Sellers in *The Gilded Age* (1873), and Jim Baker in *A Tramp Abroad* (1880), who speak in a vernacular free from prescribed standards. They remind the reader of Twain's continuing interest in good "talk" and of his belief in the honesty of the apparently unrehearsed, untutored presentation.

Twain drew on two sources for "vernacular" models. His primary inspiration was the oral tradition of the frontier—the boastful bombast of the tall-tale teller and the plain, understated style of the simple, uneducated American. In addition, he frequently praised the naïve qualities in young people's writing. He saw the fresh perceptivity of children mirrored in their composition. Thus he says in his "Complaint about Correspondents," "the most . . . interesting letters we get here from home are from children seven and eight years old . . . They write simply and naturally, and without straining for

---

a note from Twain which includes the comment: "I like the *Joan of Arc* best of all my books; & it *is* the best, I know it perfectly well" (*Mark Twain: A Biography* [New York: Harper & Brothers, 1912] II: 1034).

18. Henry Nash Smith, *Mark Twain: The Development of a Writer* (New York: Atheneum, 1967), p. 4.

effect,"[19] and in his *Autobiography* he takes pleasure in quoting lengthy passages from his daughter Suzy's biography of him.

As Twain scholars have amply documented,[20] the adventures of the outcast boy, introduced to readers in *Tom Sawyer* (1876), were a long time in the telling. Twain worked on the book intermittently over a seven-year period from 1876 to 1883. In the meantime, he produced three major works: *A Tramp Abroad* (1880), *The Prince and the Pauper* (1882), and *Life on the Mississippi* (1883). *Huck Finn* reflects his development as a novelist in these works. In *Huck* Twain returned to the "Matter of Hannibal"[21] and life on the Mississippi, subjects he explored in *Tom Sawyer* and *Life on the Mississippi*. *Huck Finn* combines burlesque with the episodic structure of travel literature, a pattern Twain exploited in *The Prince and the Pauper*. Most importantly, in *Huck Finn* Twain created a narrator with both a boy's naïveté and a social outcast's honesty. As Tanner notes, "vernacular outlaw and narrator merge, and they merge in the figure of a child."[22] Huck's narration imposed important restrictions on Twain's tendency to play with a number of narrative poses[23] while freeing him from the restriction of prescribed forms. The distance between Huck as narrator and as protagonist is relatively small since he retains essentially the same point of view in both roles. The powerful irony of the novel results from the clear distinction between narrator and author.

19. Samuel Langhorne Clemens, "A Complaint about Correspondents," in *The Celebrated Jumping Frog of Calaveras County and other Sketches* (1867; rpt. Upper Saddle River, N.J.: Literature House, 1969), p. 31.

20. Walter Blair, "When Was *Huckleberry Finn* Written?" *American Literature* 30 (1958): 1–25.

21. Smith, *Mark Twain*, p. 72.

22. Tony Tanner, *Reign of Wonder*, p. 142.

23. John C. Gerber discusses these poses in detail in "Mark Twain's Use of the Comic Pose," *PMLA* 77 (1962): 297–304, and "The Relation between Point of View and Style in the Works of Mark Twain," in *Style in Prose Fiction: English Institute Essays, 1958*, ed. with foreword by Harold C. Martin (New York: Columbia University Press, 1959), pp. 142–71.

narrator's voice

In *Huck Finn* the narrator's voice is the novel. When the voice disappears or fails to control, the novel falters. From the first sentence the reader looks to Huck to interpret his world. To consider Huck's narrative voice is to analyze the style Twain created for him and to look at three distinct relationships: Huck as narrator and Huck as character; Huck and Twain; and Huck and the other characters. Despite Huck's apparent uniqueness, he shares with the narrators of *The Bostonians* and *The Rise of Silas Lapham* a disdain for romance and an antiomniscience which surfaces as cautious accuracy.

Two aspects of Huck's style stand out—the colloquialness and the pretense of speech. As Albert Stone notes, "the vernacular language . . . in *Huckleberry Finn,* strikes the ear with the freshness of a real boy talking out loud."[24] Huck's style includes many features of direct discourse, including a casualness about how he reports the discourse of other characters. Therefore, the confusion of his direct and indirect forms is not surprising. What is surprising is that Huck can remember verbatim lengthy direct addresses (e.g., Colonel Sherburn's speech, the Duke's cannibalized *Hamlet* soliloquy). In a sense, the reader thinks of Huck as recording these events as they happen. While the novel is framed as a retrospective story, it has all the qualities of a dramatic commentary. Huck is always limited to reporting what he observes and thinks, as in Howells' "autobiographical" form, where ". . . the conditions are that you must not go outside of your own observation and experience; you cannot tell what you have not yourself seen and known to happen."[25] When Huck recounts a tall-tale

24. Albert Stone, *The Innocent Eye: Childhood in Mark Twain's Imagination* (New York: Archon Books, 1970), pp. 141–2.

25. "Novel-Writing and Novel-Reading: An Impersonal Explanation," ed. William M. Gibson in *Howells and James: A Double Billing* (New York: New York Public Library, 1958), p. 22.

about one Hank Bunker, who "got drunk and fell off of the
shot tower and spread himself out so that he was just a kind
of layer . . . and they slid him edgeways between two barn
doors for a coffin . . . ,"[26] he offers a concluding qualification
to explain his knowledge, "so they say, but I didn't see it. Pap
told me."

Critics sometimes fault Huck for not telling all that he
knows, namely, that Jim is a free man when they reach the
Phelps farm. Too much has been made of this point; it is not
a hoax or a practical joke on the reader. Huck tells his story
as he lived it; he freely swaps verb tenses and deictic markers.
The distance between his "experiencing" self and his "narrating" self[27] is insignificant. The retrospective irony of Ishmael
in *Moby-Dick* is altogether absent in *Huck Finn*. Huck is aware
of himself as a participant in the events he narrates and this
awareness adds immediacy to the text. Moreover, Huck's perspective and voice coincide, although the author and the
reader share, at times, a different perspective.

Twain makes Huck's style work by using certain vernacular
features, such as nonstandard verb forms, contractions, and
faulty subordination to create the pretense of an untutored
narrator, while at the same time developing a highly sophisticated, innovative literary style that uses a full range of standard English constructions and literary devices. This balance
creates a constant and productive tension in the text between
narrative voice and authorial control. For example, Huck
characteristically uses the conjunction *and* to link any number
of subordinate and coordinate ideas, a practice that suggests
a lack of linguistic sophistication. However, the rhythm and
parallelism that this usage establishes is a feature of the style

26. Clemens, *Huck Finn*, p. 47.
27. Dorrit Cohn notes that "the distinction between 'narrating self' (*erzählendes Ich*)
and 'experiencing self' (*erlebendes Ich*) was first made by Leo Spitzer in his essay on
Proust (*Stilstudien* II (1922, rpt. Munich 1961), p. 478." (Dorrit Cohn, *Transparent
Minds: Narrative Modes for Presenting Consciousness in Fiction* [Princeton: Princeton University Press, 1978] p. 298).

Twain is creating through Huck. In the same way, Huck has certain pet phrases like "pretty soon" and "by-and-by" that seemingly signify little more than his imprecision about time, but the way that these phrases reveal both the tempo of Huck's life and the relative importance he attaches to events is a creation of the author. *Huck Finn* offered Twain enormous freedom to indulge his linguistic imagination (the novel introduces many new words into American English) under the guise of Huck's simplicity. The reader expects Huck to have a limited vocabulary; therefore, Twain can achieve delightful metaphorical effects by having Huck use words in new grammatical functions as when he "plays another chicken bone and gets another think."[28] Twain also plays on Huck's ignorance in the confusion of similar sounding words (i.e., *diseased/deceased*).

One of the most interesting nonstandard features in Huck's voice is the way he uses verb tense. On the most obvious level, Huck's frequent substitution of present for preterit is typical both of nonstandard English and of conversation in general. In another sense, Huck's present tense takes some of his experiences and generalizes them to the habitual present,[29] as when Huck, in describing a "typical" Mississippi sunrise, tells the reader, ". . . you see the mist curl up off of the water, and the east reddens up, and you make out a log cabin in the edge of the woods. . . ."[30] Huck's present tense also identifies his involvement in the process of storytelling. He uses what Martin Joos calls "the narrative actual present" that "has a firm basis in speech, where the use of actual tense for past events comes naturally to the lips of a man who gets himself involved in what he is talking about."[31] Thus Huck tells us that "the king gets up and comes forward a little" or "the king begins

28. Clemens, *Huck Finn*, p. 138.
29. Cohn, *Transparent Minds*, p. 190.
30. Clemens, *Huck Finn*, p. 96.
31. Martin Joos, *The English Verb: Form & Meanings* (Madison: University of Wisconsin Press, 1968), p. 131.

to work his jaw again."[32] Finally, Huck uses the timeless present[33] to frame his moral judgments or his comments and generalization: "Music *is* a good thing . . ."; "Human beings *can*
be awful cruel to one another."[34] Except for these gnomic
statements, Huck does not use the present tense to step out
of his narrative and offer retrospective evaluations of the
events of the story. Only in the opening and closing paragraphs does he discuss his narrative function: "You don't
know about me . . ."; "Tom's most well, now . . . so there ain't
nothing more to write about. . . ."[35]

Twain's poeticization of Huck's linguistic idiosyncrasies
works so well because the idiosyncrasies themselves do not
overwhelm the reader. Robert Lowenherz calculates that
Twain restricted "dialect spelling to less than one percent of
Huck's narrative speech . . . consistently throughout the
novel."[36] Similarly, in revising *Huck Finn,* Twain introduced
many nonstandard features in strategic places, while regular-
izing the grammar at other points, so that the dialect and suggestions of illiterate usage "might count."[37]

Huck's opening paragraph establishes his narrative style:

> You don't know about me, without you have read a
> book by the name of "The Adventures of Tom Sawyer,"
> but that ain't no matter. That book was made by Mr. Mark
> Twain and he told the truth, mainly. There was things
> which he stretched, but mainly he told the truth. That is
> nothing. I never seen anybody but lied, one time or an-
> other, without it was Aunt Polly, or the widow, or maybe
> Mary. Aunt Polly—Tom's Aunt Polly, she is—and Mary,
> and the Widow Douglas, is all told about in that book—

32. Clemens, *Huck Finn,* p. 132.
33. Cohn, *Transparent Minds,* p. 190.
34. Clemens, *Huck Finn,* pp. 132 and 182.
35. Ibid., pp. 7 and 229.
36. Robert Lowenherz, "The Beginning of 'Huckleberry Finn,'" *American Speech*
38 (1963): 197.
37. Sydney J. Krause, "Twain's Method and Theory of Composition," *Modern Philology* 56 (1959): 176.

which is mostly a true book; with some stretchers, as I said before.[38]

Huck is unassuming; his narrative "I" does not appear until midway through the paragraph. He is more immediately concerned with "you," the reader, and with putting some distance between himself and Mr. Mark Twain, the man who "made" *Tom Sawyer.* Huck creates himself much as Silas Lapham does. We learn about Silas through Bartley's interview with him; we learn about Huck through his summary of someone else's book.

Huck's grammar in the paragraph seems strikingly non-standard, his vocabulary limited and repetitious, his presentation rambling and disorganized. Each of these devices has a literary effect. For example, Huck's double negative "but that ain't no matter" characterizes him as both illiterate and self-effacing. Moreover, it is a qualification that undermines the negativism of the opening clause. Huck makes an assertion, but he doesn't want to offend the reader. Other qualifications—"mainly," "mostly," "without it was," "with some stretchers"—are typical of Huck's style. Throughout the novel, Huck uses qualifiers in the interest of accuracy, "well, likely it was minutes and minutes."[39] Moreover, he does not want to exaggerate his own knowledge or importance, so he "reckons" a lot, and when he offers an opinion, he frequently defers to the reader: "You may say what you want to, but in my opinion. . . ."[40] In this paragraph, Huck's qualifications add up to an indictment of Twain! They also play on the primary theme of the paragraph—honesty, specifically, honesty in storytelling. The lexical repetitions of the paragraph reflect Huck's preoccupation with truth and lying, the emphasis for him is clearly in the "stretchers." In a sense, this elaborate

38. Clemens, *Huck Finn*, p. 7.
39. Ibid., p. 10.
40. Ibid., p. 152.

discussion of the "stretchers" in a book about Tom Sawyer written by Twain foreshadows the exaggeration and burlesque of *Huck Finn's* ending.

The paragraph as a whole seems to wander from topic to topic without any real sense of purpose. For instance, in the second sentence, where we might expect to get some information about the narrator, Huck launches into a digression on *The Adventures of Tom Sawyer.* He does not return to the topic of his own identity but follows his train of thought as it takes him from *Tom Sawyer* to Mark Twain to the topic of honesty in general and finally back to *The Adventures of Tom Sawyer.* Yet, the rambling organization establishes Huck's relationship with the author and the reader, making it possible for the reader to accept Huck as narrator while still being aware of the author's presence. It sets the stage for chapter 1 to detail the significant events of *Tom Sawyer,* and it "even works in some free advertisement for . . . *The Adventures of Tom Sawyer.* "[41] Moreover, it establishes within Huck's narration a potential for change—a major characteristic of conversation—and also part of Twain's theory of narrative technique. In his *Autobiography,* he notes, "narrative should flow as flows the brook down through the hills and the leafy woodlands, its course changed by every boulder it comes across."[42]

Huck's narration involves an interesting paradox rooted in his personality. His voice, his vision, and his world are constantly before the reader, but Huck actually talks very little about himself except as a participant in the events of the story. As James Cox notes: "Although Huck's language constantly describes his feelings and thoughts, they are so directly wedded to external action and dependent on it that he seems to have no independent 'thought.' "[43] Huck begins his adventures on the river by "lighting out" from his bondage to Pap,

41. Lowenherz, "Beginning of 'Huck Finn,' " p. 201.

42. Clemens, *Autobiography* I, p. 237.

43. James Cox, *Mark Twain: The Fate of Humor* (Princeton: Princeton University Press, 1966), p. 182, fn. 19.

whose drinking and violence have frightened Huck into action. Pascal Covici labels Huck's escape in chapter 7 "as active an episode as Huck engineers,"[44] and Edgar Branch compares Huck's style of narrating it to Hemingway.[45] In this paragraph Huck is actor, observer, and critic. He watches himself acting, meticulously describing the activity, and then offers an evaluation.

> I took the axe and smashed in the door—I beat it and hacked it considerable, a-doing it. I fetched the pig in and took him back nearly to the table and hacked into his throat with the axe, and laid him down on the ground to bleed—I say ground because it *was* ground—hard packed, and no boards. Well, next I took an old sack and put a lot of big rocks in it,—all I could drag—and I started it from the pig and dragged it to the door and through the woods down to the river and dumped it in, and down it sunk, out of sight. You could easy see that something had been dragged over the ground. I did wish Tom Sawyer was there, I knowed he would take an interest in this kind of business, and throw in the fancy touches. Nobody could spread himself like Tom Sawyer in such a thing as that.[46]

The paragraph's basic rhythm, one active verb after another, supports Huck's "no-nonsense" approach and suggests that apprehension leaves him no time to waste. Yet he performs each act in a methodical and deliberate way, and, despite the urgency of his activity, he demonstrates an awareness of the reader and of his own storytelling role. The qualification he addresses to the reader—"I say ground because . . ."—reflects his concern for accuracy, and the marked intersentence linkage, "well, next," varies the staccato rhythm of his description. Conversational touches

44. Pascal Covici, Jr., *Mark Twain's Humor: The Image of a World* (Dallas: Southern Methodist University Press, 1962), p. 66.

45. Edgar Marquess Branch, *The Literary Apprenticeship of Mark Twain, with Selections from His Apprentice Writing* (New York: Russell & Russell, 1966), p. 208.

46. Clemens, *Huck Finn*, p. 31.

soften the intensity of the narration and suggest the agreeable personality of the narrator. As Huck's perspective shifts from actor to observer, his vocabulary becomes less concrete and more vague, almost ambiguous: "something," "this kind of business," "such a thing as that." Through this ambiguity Twain not only simulates the mystery Huck is creating, he also shows Huck's inability to deal with abstract concepts.

Huck concludes his description by admiring his own style. Similarly, in other scenes where Huck narrates his own often frenetic activity, he is able to comment on the events as he describes them. When Pap chases him around the cabin and Huck believes he is going to be killed, he comments: ". . . I thought I was gone; but I slid out of the jacket quick as lightning, and saved myself."[47] When he is about to be incriminated in the King and Duke's sham at the Wilks's, he is again near death, but he accompanies the description of his escape with the comment ". . . the way I lit out and shinned for the road in the dark, there ain't nobody can tell."[48] Even in crisis situations he maintains his storytelling pose which transforms him from character to narrator.

In his description of nature, Huck's style is particularly innovative. Twain had been troubled throughout his writing career with the conventional literary models for presenting nature. When he describes his native landscape in *Life on the Mississippi,* he distinguishes, as Leo Marx says, between the "sentimental views of the passengers and the analytical attitude of the pilot, between a lush picture and mere matters of fact."[49] Huck's narration enabled Twain to merge reverence and knowledge. Huck has not lost his ability to wonder

47. Ibid., p. 28.
48. Ibid., p. 161.
49. Leo Marx, "The Pilot and the Passenger: Landscape Conventions and the Style of *Huckleberry Finn,"American Literature* 28 (1956), rpt. in *Mark Twain: A Collection of Critical Essays,* ed. Henry Nash Smith (Englewood Cliffs, N.J.: Prentice-Hall, 1963), p. 52.

and to describe each experience with fresh insight; at the same time, he is wise in nature's ways and alert to the details of every situation. Moreover, he is never a passive observer: the nature he admires affects him intimately. He is always inside his picture, never detached or aloof.

More critical attention has been devoted to Huck's description of the sunrise on the river at the beginning of chapter 19 than to any other passage in *Huck Finn*. Kenneth Lynn reflects the opinions of other critics when he says, "Huck's description of the sunrise . . . is one of the two or three most perfectly controlled pieces of descriptive prose in American literature."[50]

> Two or three days and nights went by; I reckon I might say they swum by, they slid along so quiet and smooth and lovely. Here is the way we put in the time. It was a monstrous big river down there—sometimes a mile and a half wide; we run nights, and laid up and hid day-times; soon as night was most gone, we stopped navigating and tied up—nearly always in the dead water under a tow-head; and then cut young cottonwoods and willows and hid the raft with them. Then we set out the lines. Next we slid into the river and had a swim, so as to freshen up and cool off; then we set down on the sandy bottom where the water was about knee deep, and watched the daylight come. Not a sound anywheres—perfectly still—just like the whole world was asleep, only sometimes the bullfrogs a-cluttering, maybe. The first thing to see, looking away over the water, was a kind of dull line—that was the woods on t'other side—you couldn't make nothing else out; then a pale place in the sky; then more paleness, spreading around, then the river softened up, away off, and warn't black any more, but gray; you could see little dark spots drifting along, ever so far away—trading scows, and such things; and long black streaks—rafts;

50. Kenneth Lynn, *Mark Twain and Southwestern Humor* (Boston: Little, Brown, and Co., 1959), p. 223.

sometimes you could hear a sweep screaking; or jumbled up voices, it was so still, and sounds come so far; and by-and-by you could see a streak on the water which you know by the look of the streak that there's a snag there in a swift current which breaks on it and makes that streak look that way; and you see the mist curl up off of the water, and the east reddens up, and the river, and you make out a log cabin in the edge of the woods, away on the bank on t'other side of the river, being a wood-yard, likely, and piled by them cheats so you can throw a dog through it anywheres; then the nice breeze springs up, and comes fanning you from over there, so cool and fresh, and sweet to smell, on account of the woods and the flowers; but sometimes not that way, because they've left dead fish laying around, gars, and such, and they do get pretty rank; and next you've got the full day, and everything smiling in the sun, and the song-birds just going it![51]

Twain creates a generalized picture through Huck's verb forms. In the middle of the paragraph, a sentence fragment—"not a sound anywheres"—interrupts the pattern of past-tense verbs. Huck moves into the scene, breaking down barriers of time and place. The deliberate vagueness of the subject of the infinitive "to see" in the first clause of sentence seven brings the reader into the scene. The viewer might be either the "I" or "we" of the preceding sentences or the generalized impersonal "you" of succeeding clauses. When Huck reintroduces finite verbs in seven, many are *could* constructions—"you could see," "you could hear." The *could* preterits, suggesting repeated activity, coupled with the impersonal *you,* generalize the response and imply the unstated condition—"whenever you were there or whenever you saw this sight." Ultimately, the sense that this is a composite scene does not depend entirely on verb structure;

51. Clemens, *Huck Finn,* p. 96.

Huck begins by talking about several days and nights. Within the body of his description, his digression about the cheats on shore—"but sometimes not that way, because they've left dead fish laying around"—also indicates that this scene encompasses more than one occasion.

Rhythm is by far the most important rhetorical device in the passage, and Twain maintains Huck's easy, casual pace with two-part colloquial verbs and many prepositions: "slid along," "freshen up," "softened up away off," "curl up off of." Huck's habit of using conjunctions between every item in a series helps to keep the pace even and unhurried—"so quiet and smooth and lovely," "so cool and fresh and sweet." His frequent use of present participles as post-nominal adjectives adds to the rhythm, evoking a sense of the river's lulling motion and providing a form of repetition that contributes to the aural organization of the passage. For instance, Huck describes "the bull-frogs a-cluttering," "the paleness spreading around," "little dark spots drifting along," "the song-birds just going it." Finally, some of Huck's characteristic locutions enhance the rhythm, as in the first sentence where he says, "I reckon I might say they swum by."

In a general way, the syntax of the entire passage is symbolic. As Huck's eye picks up one change after another in the scene, fragmentary phrases involving both disjunction and ellipsis like "then a pale place in the sky; then more paleness spreading around," "and long black streaks—rafts," follow one another, often separated from their subjects and verbs by intervening objects, yet Huck's meaning is never in doubt. He makes no attempt to organize his impressions thematically. Instead, his orientation is entirely temporal and spatial, supported by the loosely coordinated syntax. When Huck says "and the east reddens up, and the river, and you make out . . . ," no one idea is subordinate to another, and the coordination itself is incomplete.

The passage involves a remarkable balance between the poetic use of language, supported by numerous rhetorical devices, such as the syntactic symbolism just described,[52] and the practical specificity of Huck's voice. Huck's vocabulary captures the particular details of the scene. *Bull-frogs* not just frogs *clutter; trading-scows* drift along; Huck and Jim cut *cotton-woods* and *willows* not just trees; a *sweep,* not a bird, *screaks;* and the dead fish are "gars, and such." When Huck uses vague phrases, like the just quoted "and such," the details seem unimportant to him. As Clerc notes, a "tension . . . between definiteness or exactness and inexactness and approximations"[53] pervades the passage. Although Huck speaks authoritatively on some points, his frequent use of qualifications—*likely, most, about, nearly, maybe, sometimes, pretty*—reflect his unwillingness to impose absolutes on a constantly changing scene. Whereas Howells' narrator hedges his evaluations of characters and events, Huck's qualifications reveal the unreliability of a world beyond his control. Huck's knowledge and honesty create a nonromanticized presentation. At the same time, however, he has not lost the sense of wonder that is present from the moment he and Jim sit reverentially in the stillness waiting for the spectacular scene to unfold.

When Huck describes his own activity or an event in nature, Twain seems most able to balance his art with the artlessness of Huck's voice. Twain's authorial control is more conspicuous in the accounts of Huck's social interaction. Henry Nash Smith divides the novel into three parts: "the story of Huck and Jim's adventures in their flight toward freedom"; "the social satire of the towns along the river"; and "the developing characterization of Huck."[54] Smith notes that "throughout the long middle section, while he [Huck] is primarily an observer, . . . he is endowed with Mark Twain's own unambiguous attitude toward the fraud and folly he witnesses."[55]

---

52. Charles Clerc offers an extensive description of the passage's rhetorical devices in "Sunrise on the River: 'The Whole World' of Huckleberry Finn," *Modern Fiction Studies* 14 (Spring, 1968): 67–78.

53. Ibid., p. 74.

54. Smith, *Mark Twain,* p. 114.

55. Ibid., p. 119.

Occasionally Twain brings the "fraud and folly" into focus at the expense of Huck's narration. While first-person narrators are traditionally allowed the liberty of "perfect recall,"[56] a few sequences in *Huck Finn,* most notably the Duke's version of Hamlet's soliloquy[57] and Colonel Sherburn's "half-a'man" address to the lynch mob,[58] stretch the reader's indulgence, particularly because they seem to be quoted out of proportion to Huck's interest in them. Smith comments that "the Sherburn episode seems unusually isolated. None of the principal characters is involved in or affected by it . . . and Huck is a spectator whom even the author hardly notices."[59] By comparison, Pap's rather lengthy diatribe against the "govment"[60] seems to belong in the novel and in Huck's memory. It develops Pap's character, as town drunk, petty philosopher, and racist, and it is likely that Huck has heard some version of the speech on many occasions: "Whenever his liquor begun to work, he most always went for the govment."[61]

A more subtle indication of authorial intrusion occurs when Huck's descriptions exceed his linguistic and intellectual capacity. J. R. Boggan notes the Darwinian overtone of Huck's description of Pap just prior to his "govment" speech: "A body would a thought he was Adam, he was just all mud."[62] Huck seems to overextend his narrative capacities most often in his descriptions of society where Twain

56. Bertil Romberg, *Studies in the Narrative Technique of the First-Person Novel* (Lund, Sweden: Almqvist & Wiksell, 1962), p. 97. Franz Stanzel explains the convention without naming it: "The narrator, who stands at a great temporal distance, is permitted to reproduce long dialogues as direct quotations although such a feat of memory is beyond what is humanly possible" (Franz Stanzel, *Narrative Situations in the Novel: Tom Jones, Moby-Dick, The Ambassadors, Ulysses* [Bloomington and London: Indiana University Press, 1971], p. 72).

57. Clemens, *Huck Finn*, p. 111.

58. Ibid., pp. 118–19.

59. Smith, *Mark Twain*, p. 135.

60. Clemens, *Huck Finn*, p. 60.

61. Ibid., p. 26.

62. J. R. Boggan, "That Slap, Huck, Did It Hurt?" *English Language Notes* 1 (March, 1964): 215.

makes him the mouthpiece for his own social satire. When
Huck describes a girl in one of Emmaline Grangerford's pictures as wearing "very *wee* black slippers" and "leaning *pensive*
on a tombstone . . . her other hand hanging down her side
holding . . . a *reticule*" (italics mine),[63] the reader may wonder
momentarily where Huck got this vocabulary. Similarly one
may question the appropriateness of some of the phrases
Huck uses to describe the circus bareback riders: "lovely complexion," "most loveliest parasol."[64] As George Mayberry
notes, " 'the most loveliest parasol' . . . is not the primitive
poet in Huck, but the overreaching artist in Samuel Langhorne Clemens. . . ."[65] By contrast, Huck tells us that the men
were "just in their drawers and undershirts." Finally, when
Huck recounts the King's "tears and flapdoodle" speech, he
says the King "blubbers out a pious goody-goody Amen."[66]
Goody-goody seems to be Huck's; *pious* is Twain's added lick.

One form of "alleged" authorial intrusion in Huck's narration is difficult to prove. Louis Rubin, following Smith, notes
that on occasion Huck acts as "the author's surrogate."[67]
Huck's reactions in certain situations "enable him [Twain] to
identify his own feelings with Huck's."[68] So, for example,
Huck's depression as he approaches the Phelps farm where
Jim is held prisoner seems to some critics to be disproportion-
ate to the difficulty Huck anticipates in freeing Jim. Rubin
concludes: "When encountering such a passage the reader
senses, therefore, that Huck is expressing his author's attitudes, and that these attitudes, however much the situation
itself may be contained in the plot structure, come from Mark
Twain's life and memories."[69] Smith provides ample evidence

63. Clemens, *Huck Finn*, p. 84.
64. Ibid., p. 119.
65. George Mayberry, "Reading and Writing," *New Republic,* 7 May 1944, p. 608.
66. Clemens, *Huck Finn*, p. 132.
67. Louis D. Rubin, Jr., *The Teller in the Tale* (Seattle: University of Washington
Press, 1967), p. 56.
68. Ibid., p. 68.
69. Ibid., p. 70.

from Twain's other writing to substantiate this claim,[70] but neither the language itself nor even the subject matter creates the effect. Huck's description of the farm's lonesome atmosphere reminds the reader of his feelings at Miss Watson's in the first chapter. The same "Sunday-like" atmosphere pervades both scenes. Twain is, in fact, closing the book's frame and bringing Huck back to "dismal" civilization. Twain himself may regret the end of Huck and Jim's journey, but so, too, does Huck. The voice is Huck's even if the sentiments are Twain's.

By contrast, in the scene preceding his arrival at the Phelps place, Huck's argument with his conscience and his final decision—"All right, then, I'll *go* to hell"[71]—do violate the consistency of his narrative voice. Huck's initial reaction to finding Jim gone is to feel sorry for Jim and for himself over the loss of Jim. He decides to write to Miss Watson because it would be better for Jim to be a slave at home. He then decides that Jim would only be miserable at home, and more importantly, by revealing himself as Jim's companion, he would bring shame on himself for having helped a slave escape. His conscience intrudes to justify society's condemnation of him:

> And at last, when it hit me all of a sudden that here was the plain hand of Providence slapping me in the face and letting me know my wickedness was being watched all the time from up there in heaven, whilst I was stealing a poor old woman's nigger that hadn't ever done me no harm, and now was showing me there's One that's always on the lookout, and ain't agoing to allow no such miserable doings to go only just so fur and no further; I most dropped in my tracks I was so scared.[72]

70. Smith, *Mark Twain*, pp. 129–31.
71. Clemens, *Huck Finn*, p. 169.
72. Ibid., p. 168.

Huck goes on to discuss his lack of Sunday-school education, and he tries to pray for himself.

For Huck to argue with himself using these stock religious phrases contradicts his character. As George Carrington notes: ". . . from cultural analysis Huck turns to brooding about his conscience and what he should have learned but did not learn at Sunday school, and with this the episode falls down . . . The transition is handled smoothly, but it is Twain doing the manipulating, not Huck. . . ."[73] In fact, Huck has been through these arguments about the "immorality" of helping Jim earlier in the novel in chapter 16, but the religious issue does not surface there. ". . . Not until the thirty-first chapter does Huck suddenly get religion, fear God."[74]

Very early in the novel Huck has made short work of the advantages of prayer, Sunday school, and Providence. He tries prayer and determines ". . . there ain't nothing in it."[75] Huck shows his contempt for Sunday school when he dismisses Tom Sawyer's romantic imagination, particularly his belief in genies coming out of lamps, as having "all the marks of a Sunday school."[76] On the subject of Providence he concludes: "I judged I could see that there was two Providences, and a poor chap would stand considerable show with the widow's Providence, but if Miss Watson's got him there warn't no help for him any more."[77] In Huck's debate over Jim, he confronts himself with Miss Watson's not the widow's Providence. Miss Watson's is "always on the lookout" for wickedness; it is the power that enforces conventional morality. Huck's invocation of this Providence against himself has a hollow ring; it becomes a conceit Twain

73. George C. Carrington, Jr., *The Dramatic Unity of "Huckleberry Finn"* (Columbus: Ohio State University Press, 1976), p. 144.

74. Boggan, "That Slap," p. 121.

75. Clemens, *Huck Finn*, p. 15.

76. Ibid., p. 17.

77. Ibid., p. 15.

develops to make for a more dramatic conflict within Huck.

A few other elements in the presentation of the scene suggest that once Twain got going in Huck's speech, the drama of the event rather than the need for narrative consistency won out. One of the virtues of Huck's character is that he is nondidactic; he does not deliver the obvious conclusions to the reader. As Perry Miller notes, ". . . he never draws the moral, he lets the language show what is better left unsaid."[78] But after Huck gets going on the religious theme, an unnaturally exhortatory tone creeps in. Huck tries to pray and the words won't come. He then engages in some rather wordy rhetorical posturing:

> Why wouldn't they? It warn't no use to try and hide it from Him. Nor from *me,* neither. I knowed very well why they wouldn't come. It was because my heart warn't right; it was because I warn't square; it was because I was playing double.[79]

The vocabulary—"warn't," "square," "playing double"—is Huck's, but the use of a rhetorical question and the parallel repetitions with their sermon-like stress are alien to him, as is the outright statement of a moral, "You can't pray a lie," which ends the paragraph.

Ultimately, when Huck's "sound heart" wins out over his conscience, he decides "I'll *go* to hell," and Perry Miller tells us that in "this defiance . . . we have the plain style triumphant."[80] Although Huck's statement dramatizes a painful moral lesson, it seems to lack the necessary reticence Miller attributes to the plain style, and it contradicts the spirit and tone of the memories that prompt it. As Cox says, "the decision . . . is cast in the positive locution of Tom Sawyer, not

78. Miller, *Nature's Nation,* p. 235.
79. Clemens, *Huck Finn,* p. 168.
80. Miller, *Nature's Nation,* p. 231.

in Huck's essentially negative vernacular."[81] The authorial personality eclipses the narrator, and subsequent developments in the novel show Huck's narrative control faltering as he recounts Twain's burlesque.

Huck's narrative voice derives from his characterization. He is more than a mouthpiece for the author; his personality requires Twain to work with him as much as through him. But Huck's narration tends to be most consistent and natural when he and his world are the focus of the narrative. When Huck's relation to his subject matter is strained, as in passages describing shore life, his narrative control breaks down. The very simplicity of Huck's style invites parody. As long as Huck controls the situation and his material is sufficiently demanding, Twain maintains the flexibility and credibility of Huck's style. However, when the material does not demand that the basically simple style be innovative in order to capture complex and significant scenes and ideas, the temptations inherent in simplicity take over.

directly reported discourse

Mark Twain's prefatorial note to *Huck Finn* speaks eloquently for his attention to his characters' voices.

> In this book a number of dialects are used, to wit: the Missouri negro dialect; the extremest form of the backwoods South-Western dialect; the ordinary "Pike-County" dialect; and four modified varieties of this last. The shadings have not been done in a hap-hazard fashion, or by guess-work; but pains-takingly, and with the trustworthy guidance and support of personal familiarity with these several forms of speech.[82]

At the same time, his "explanation" of the explanation is so

81. Cox, *Mark Twain*, p. 182.
82. Clemens, *Huck Finn*, p. 2.

tongue-in-cheek as to cast doubt on his whole claim to verisimilitude.

> I make this explanation for the reason that without it many readers would suppose that all these characters were trying to talk alike and not succeeding.[83]

Basically Twain's note testifies to his interest in language as a reflection of character and setting. Of his three major dialects, two are regional—"backwoods South-Western," presumably from the Phelps's farm area, and "the ordinary 'Pike-County' dialect," of which Huck's voice is a variation. One is regional and social, "the Missouri negro," and accounts for the differences between Huck and Jim's speech. Within the Pike-County form, there are "four modified varieties." It is enough for us to note that Miss Watson, Judge Thatcher, and even Tom Sawyer speak a little differently than Huck and Pap. The accuracy of Twain's dialect is less significant than the consistency of his distinctions.[84]

Huck's marginal literacy and the limitations of his first-person perspective make it improbable that he could recall and record as much DD as he does. On at least one occasion, Huck comments on this problem. When the real Wilks relatives arrive from England and confront the Duke and King, Huck prefaces his report of one of their speeches with the comment: "I can't give the old gent's words, nor I can't imi-

83. Ibid.

84. Two articles by Lee Pederson deal with the authenticity of Twain's dialects based on analyses of the actual linguistic usage in the locations Twain purports to represent: "Negro Speech in the Adventures of Huckleberry Finn," *The Mark Twain Journal* 13, No. 1 (1965): 1–4; "Mark Twain's Missouri Dialects: Marion County Phonemics," *American Speech* 42 (1967): 261–78. Curt M. Rulon also discusses the topic in his "Geographical Delimitation of the Dialect Areas in *The Adventures of Huckleberry Finn,*" *The Mark Twain Journal* 14, No. 1, (1967): 9–12. These articles are by no means definitive. Pederson's data is exclusively phonological and is limited to informants from Marion County, Missouri; Rulon discusses only selected linguistic features. He goes into greater detail in "The Dialects in *Huckleberry Finn*" (Ph.D. dissertation, University of Iowa, 1967).

tate him; but he turned around to the crowd, and says, about like this: . . . ."[85] However, in general, the dialogues in *Huck Finn* are lively and significant. They contribute to the plot as well as provide important aspects of characterization. Moreover, they reflect Huck's careful attention to detail. When he is a participant in a conversation, he provides fewer tags than when he is describing a conversation he overhears. If he is involved, he has less opportunity to observe and record. The tags he does use describe the physical actions accompanying the talk or occasionally the impact a statement has on the other participant.

As with all the language in *Huck Finn,* the directly reported discourse reflects Twain's concern for realistic representation. The dialogues contain many clipped forms—responses are rarely complete sentences unless they involve questions or counterspeeches. Characters forget what they have just heard or said and repeat themselves. They interrupt and correct one another and they assume turn-taking roles that parallel their social roles. One of the best constructed dialogues in the novel is a conversation between the Duke and the King after their Wilks scam collapses and they have escaped the town and returned to the raft. The gold that they stole and Huck hid in Wilks's coffin excites so much interest when it is discovered that the scoundrels are able to flee, but neither of them knows how the gold got there. Huck is, of course, a silent party to their conversation; his fate rests on how they resolve the issue.

> They was still a minute—thinking—then the king says, kind of absent-minded like:
> "Mf! And we reckoned the *niggers* stole it!"
> That made me squirm!
> "Yes," says the duke, kinder slow, and deliberate, and sarcastic, "*We* did."
> After about a half a minute, the king drawls out:

85. Clemens, *Huck Finn,* p. 155.

"Leastways—*I* did."

The duke says, the same way:

"On the contrary—*I* did."

The king kind of ruffles up, and says:

"Looky here, Bilgewater, what'r you referrin' to?"

The duke says, pretty brisk:

"When it comes to that, maybe you'll let me ask, what was *you* referring to?"

"Shucks!" says the king, very sarcastic; "but *I* don't know—maybe you was asleep, and didn't know what you was about."

The duke bristles right up, now, and says:

"Oh, let *up* on this cussed nonsense—do you take me for a blame' fool? Don't you reckon *I* know who hid that money in that coffin?"

"*Yes,* sir! I know you *do* know—because you done it yourself!"

"It's a lie!"—and the duke went for him. The king sings out:

"Take y'r hands off!—leggo my throat!—I take it all back!" The duke says:

"Well, you just own up, first that you *did* hide that money there, intending to give me the slip one of these days, and come back and dig it up, and have it all to yourself."

"Wait jest a minute, duke—answer me this one question, honest and fair; if you didn't put the money there, say it, and I'll b'lieve you, and take back everything I said."

"You old scoundrel, I didn't, and you know I didn't. There, now!"

"Well, then, I b'lieve you. But answer me only jest this one more—now *don't* git mad; didn't you have it in your *mind* to hook the money and hide it?"

The duke never said nothing for a little bit; then he says:

"Well—I don't care if I *did,* I didn't *do* it, anyways. But you not only had it in mind to do it, but you *done* it."

"I wisht I may never die if I done it, duke, and that's

honest. I won't say I warn't *goin'* to do it, because I *was;* but you—I mean somebody—got in ahead o' me."

"It's a lie! You done it, and you got to *say* you done it, or—"

The king begun to gurgle, and then he gasps out: "'Nough!—I *own up!*"

I was very glad to hear him say that, it made me feel much more easier than what I was feeling before. So the duke took his hands off, and says:

"If you ever deny it again, I'll drown you. It's *well* for you to set there and blubber like a baby—it's fitten for you, after the way you've acted. I never see such an old ostrich for wanting to gobble everything—and I a trusting you all the time, like you was my own father. You ought to been ashamed of yourself to stand by and hear it saddled onto a lot of poor niggers and you never say a word for 'em. It makes me feel ridiculous to think I was soft enough to *believe* that rubbage. Cuss you, I can see, now, why you was so anxious to make up the deffesit—you wanted to get what money I'd got out of the Nonesuch and one thing or another, and scoop it *all!*" The king says, timid, and still a snuffling:

"Why duke, it was you that said make up the deffersit, it warn't me."

"Dry up! I don't want to hear no more *out* of you!" says the duke. "And *now* you see what you *got* by it. They've got all their own money back, and all of *ourn* but a shekel or two, *besides*. G'long to bed—and don't you deffersit *me* no more deffersits, long's *you* live!"[86]

This dialogue and the accompanying fight result in a confession that is contrary to fact, but the confession gets Huck off the hook. Throughout the interchange, heavy with pregnant pauses, the reader shares Huck's tension about the outcome. Huck's tags, "kind of absent-minded like," "kinder slow, and deliberate, and sarcastic," "kind of ruffles up,"

86. Ibid., pp. 164–65.

"pretty brisk," "bristles right up," involve careful observation combined with understatement to catch the nuances of sarcasm, indignation, and anger as the two participants become increasingly frustrated with one another. Only one word, *sarcasm,* seems a little sophisticated for Huck.

The interchange epitomizes the relationship between the Duke and King. The King, a masterful bluffer, is easily "squashed" and reduced to blubbering. The younger man, tougher physically and mentally, not only extracts the bogus confession but hypocritically lectures the King for letting the theft be laid off on "a lot of poor niggers" (shortly after this exchange, the Duke and King sell Jim for forty dollars) and blames the King for the idea of making up "the deffersit." The Duke's play on *deficit*—" 'don't you deffersit *me* no more deffersits' "—is double-edged. Not only does the Duke not want the King to bring it up again, for the Duke knows it was his own idea in the first place, he also does not want to be "put in the red" again by another such idea. Huck spells it three different ways in the text—" 'deffirsit,' "[87] " 'deffesit,' " and " 'deffersit.' "[88] In this conversation either the Duke's pronunciation changes to mock the King, or Huck simply records the two uses differently. The dialogue as a whole adds information to the plot, resolving the stolen gold issue, and develops the characterization.

In a first-person narrative, one of the ways a narrator creates himself as character is through direct reports of his own discourse, which seems to present him more objectively. But Huck's direct discourse most often demonstrates his skill in assuming duplicitous roles. He usually reports his straightforward conversations indirectly, reserving DD for the dramatic scenes in which he has to lie his way out of tight places. Huck's lies are not games, like Tom Sawyer's; they are a matter of survival. His direct reports force the reader to live through

87. Ibid., p. 133.
88. Ibid., p. 165.

the tension of seeing whether the ruse will work while allowing
the reader to admire Huck's "style." Huck often deals with difficult situations by assuming the pose of an innocent child; he
tells a variety of pitiful tales in which he is an orphan or near to
being one, as when his family is supposedly trapped on the
"Walter Scott" wreck. But Huck can also pretend to lie and
play on his apparent ineptness. When slave-hunters approach
the raft, he lets on that he has a family with smallpox aboard by
trying to avoid telling the men about it:

> "Pap'll be mighty much obleeged to you, I can tell you.
> Everybody goes away when I want them to help me tow
> the raft ashore, and I can't do it by myself."
> "Well, that's infernal mean. Odd, too. Say, boy, what's
> the matter with your father?"
> "It's the—a—the—well, it ain't anything, much." They
> stopped pulling. It warn't but a mighty little way to the
> raft, now. One says:
> "Boy, that's a lie. What *is* the matter with your pap? An-
> swer up square, now, and it'll be the better for you."
> "I will, sir, I will, honest—but don't leave us, please.
> It's the—the—gentlemen, if you'll only pull ahead, and
> let me heave you the head-line, you won't have to come
> a-near the raft—please do."
> "Set her back, John, set her back!" says one. They
> backed water. "Keep away, boy—keep to looard. Con-
> found I just expect the wind has blowed it to us. Your
> pap's got the small-pox, and you know it precious well.
> Why didn't you come out and say so? Do you want to
> spread it all over?"
> "Well," says I, a-blubbering, "I've told everybody be-
> fore, and then they just went away and left us."[89]

His style in this exchange is very civilized; he is exceedingly
polite and his language reflects very few colloquial characteristics. He gropes for words and appears to be incapable of car-

89. Ibid., p. 75.

rying off the simplest deceit. This "childish" Huck can burst into tears as easily as the King when a performance demands it.

In a few significant scenes, Huck *is* a child rather than feigning childishness, and his language reflects his relationship to the adult world. His first conversation with Pap captures his fear, bravado, and sullenness. When Pap breaks into Huck's room at the widow's, he and Huck have a silent stand-off, then Pap says:

> "Starchy clothes—very. You think you're a good deal of a big-bug, *don't* you?"
>
> "Maybe I am, maybe I ain't," says I.
>
> "Don't you give me none o' your lip," says he. "You've put on considerable many frills since I been away. I'll take you down a peg before I get done with you. You're educated, too, they say; can read and write. You think you're better'n your father, now, don't you, because he can't? *I*'ll take it out of you. Who told you you might meddle with such hifalut'n foolishness, hey?—who told you you could?"
>
> "The widow. She told me."
>
> "The widow, hey?—and who told the widow she could put in her shovel about a thing that ain't none of her business?"
>
> "Nobody never told her."
>
> "Well, I'll learn her how to meddle. . . ."[90]

Pap tests Huck's reading ability, tears up one of his school prizes, and returns to the fray.

> He set there a-mumbling and a-growling a minute, and then he says—
>
> "*Ain't* you a sweet-scented dandy, though? A bed; and bed-clothes, and a look'n-glass; and a piece of carpet on the floor—and your own father got to sleep with the hogs in the tanyard. I never see such a son. I bet I'll take some o' these frills out o' you before I'm done with you. Why

90. Ibid., p. 21.

there ain't no end to your airs—they say you're rich. Hey?—how's that?"

"They lie—that's how."

"Looky here—mind how you talk to me; I'm a-standing about all I can stand, now—so don't gimme no sass. I've been in town two days, and I hain't heard nothing but about you bein' rich. I heard about it away down the river, too. That's why I come. You git me that money to-morrow—I want it."

"I hain't got no money."

"It's a lie. Judge Thatcher's got it. You git it. I want it."

"I hain't got no money, I tell you. You ask Judge Thatcher; he'll tell you the same."

"All right. I'll ask him; and I'll make him pungle, too, or I'll know the reason why. Say—how much you got in your pocket? I want it."

"I hain't got only a dollar, and I want that to—"

"It don't make no difference what you want it for—you just shell it out."[91]

Huck's initial response is cocky, but he quickly retreats into a tight-lipped appeal to authority: "The widow. She told me." He regains some of his resourcefulness and decides to deny his treasure but his attempt is half-hearted and belligerent. He doesn't spin any tales for Pap; he appeals again to a local authority, Judge Thatcher; and he fails to protect his dollar with a lie. Pap is cruel and dangerous, and Huck doesn't have much confidence in his own ability to delude him until he hits upon his elaborate escape plan.

A number of dialogues in the novel reveal Twain's pleasure in language play, and while they deepen the characterization, they are largely irrelevant to the plot. When Huck has his dinner conversation with the youngest Wilks sister, Joanna, she traps him repeatedly in lies about his "English" life. Joanna's dogged grilling finds Huck looking for daylight to get "out of the woods."

91. Ibid., pp. 21–22.

Next, she says:

"Do you go to church, too?"

"Yes—regular."

"Where do you set?"

"Why, in our pew."

"*Whose* pew?"

"Why, *ourn*—your Uncle Harvey's."

"His'n? What does *he* want with a pew?"

"Wants it to set in. What did you *reckon* he wanted with it?"

"Why, I thought he'd be in the pulpit."

Rot him, I forgot he was a preacher. I see I was up a stump again, so I played another chicken bone and got another think.[92]

Twain loves the sparring and invents new ways for Huck to describe his dilemma, as when he plays "another chicken bone." Earlier Huck has "let on to get choked with a chicken bone, so as to get time to think how to get down again."[93]

Occasionally these verbal games have significance beyond the mere display of verbal resourcefulness. When Huck and Jim argue about why Frenchmen speak a different language, Huck appears to be the sophisticate playing off of Jim's innocence. But although Huck, as narrator, has the last word, the reader can see that Jim bests him in the argument.

"Looky here, Jim; does a cat talk like we do?"

"No, a cat don't."

"Well, does a cow?"

"No, a cow don't, nuther."

"Does a cat talk like a cow, or a cow talk like a cat?"

"No, dey don't."

"It's natural and right for 'em to talk different from each other, ain't it?"

"Course."

92. Ibid., p. 138.
93. Ibid., p. 137.

"And ain't it natural and right for a cat and a cow to talk different from *us?*"

"Why, mos' sholy it is."

"Well, then, why ain't it natural and right for a *Frenchman* to talk different from us? You answer me that."

"Is a cat a man, Huck?"

"No."

"Well, den dey ain't no sense in a cat talkin' like a man. Is a cow a man?—er is a cow a cat?"

"No, she ain't either of them."

"Well, den she ain' got no business to talk like either one er the yuther of 'em. Is a Frenchman a man?"

"Yes."

"*Well,* den! Dad blame it, why doan' he *talk* like a man? You answer me *dat!*"

I see it warn't no use wasting words—you can't learn a nigger to argue. So I quit.[94]

Finally, there is the incredible ingenuity of the dialogues at the Phelps farm after Tom and Huck help Jim escape. The romantic insanity of Tom's scheme seems quite literally to have driven the townspeople mad, if their speech is any index. Huck introduces this lengthy dialogue with the explanation:

And the place was plumb full of farmers and farmers' wives, to dinner; and such a clack a body never heard. Old Mrs. Hotchkiss was the worst; her tongue was agoing all the time. She says:

"Well, Sister Phelps, I've ransacked that-air cabin over an' I b'lieve the nigger was crazy. I says so to Sister Damrell—didn't I, Sister Damrell?—s'I, he's crazy, s'I—them's the very words I said. You all hearn me: he's crazy, s'I; everything shows it, s'I. Look at that-air grindstone, s'I; want to tell *me* 't any cretur 'ts in his right mind 's agoin' to scrabble all them crazy things onto a grindstone, s'I? Here sich 'n' sich a person busted his heart; 'n' here so 'n' so pegged along for thirty-seven year, 'n' all that—

94. Ibid., p. 67.

natcherl son o' Louis somebody 'n' sich everlast'n rubbage. He's plumb crazy, s'I; it's what I says in the fust
place, it's what I says in the middle, 'n' it's what I says last
'n' all the time—the nigger's crazy—crazy's Nebokood-
neezer, s'I."

"An' look at that-air ladder made out'n rags, Sister
Hotchkiss," says old Mrs. Damrell, "what in the name o'
goodness *could* he ever want of—"

"The very words I was a-sayin' no longer ago th'n this
minute to Sister Utterback, 'n' she'll tell you so herself.
Sh-she, look at that-air rag ladder, sh-she; 'n' s'I, yes, *look*
at it, s'I—what *could* he a wanted of it, s'I. Sh-she, Sister
Hotchkiss, sh-she—"

"But how in the nation'd they ever *git* that grindstone
in there, *any*way? 'n' who dug that-air *hole?* 'n' who—"

"My very *words* Brer Penrod! I was a-sayin'—pass that-
air sasser o' m'lasses, won't ye?—I was a-sayin' to Sister
Dunlap, jist this minute, how *did* they git that grindstone
in there, s'I. Without *help*, mind you—'thout *help! Thar's*
wher' tis. Don't tell *me*, s'I; there *wuz* help, s'I; 'n' ther'
wuz a *plenty* help, too, s'I; ther's ben a *dozen* a-helpin' that
nigger, 'n' I lay I'd skin every last nigger on this place,
but *I'd* find out who done it, s'I; 'n' moreover, s'I—"

"A *dozen* says you!—*forty* couldn't a-done everything
that's been done. Look at them case-knife saws and
things, how tedious they've been made; look at that bed-
leg sawed off with 'em, a week's work for six men; look
at that nigger made out'n straw on the bed; and look
at—"[95]

This conversation continues with the Brothers and Sisters
interrupting one another and the reader getting little guid-
ance from Huck about the identity of the speakers until finally
Sister Phelps gives her account of the terror the family has
lived through. While superficially the talk caricatures the
country people and their gossipy ways, it has a number of un-

95. Ibid., pp. 218–19.

derlying themes. It demonstrates how powerfully Tom's plan
has worked on the provincial imagination. Carrington summarizes the sequence: "Here is pure chaos, experienced, reported, discussed, and turned into legend, the most durable
form of drama."[96] It testifies to the Herculean efforts that
Tom, Jim, and Huck have expended on this charade. Finally,
it captures the fears of a society in which the slave owners can
credit the "simple" slaves with such a complicated and apparently sophisticated plan. Though the discourse is, as Bridgman says, "verbal inventiveness of a very high order,"[97] it is
Twain's inventiveness, not Huck's. Although Huck is interested in these reactions because he is concerned for Jim and
Tom's safety, he would not need to give the reader such a de-
tailed record. Twain has created an opportunity to experiment with dialogue and dialect. The innovative results may
justify the authorial intrusion, but this dialogue, unlike the
previous ones cited, eclipses Huck and his story.

Occasionally, Huck omits quotation marks from what is obviously direct discourse. In the midst of an indirect report of
Jim's speech, Huck drops in the sentence "I says, go on,"[98]
clearly a direct discourse form. Doležel calls this type of report unmarked direct discourse (UDD), "a variant of DD
which preserves all the grammatical, semantic and speech-
level features of DD, but lacks its demarcation marks (the conventional punctuation of DD)."[99] Huck frequently uses UDD
to record his "thoughts," which, with the exception of his rehearsal of the river journey in chapter 31, are always direct
addresses to himself or to the reader.

Although Twain eliminates the cumbersome barrier of
quotation marks in presenting these thoughts, they have the

96. Carrington, *Dramatic Unity*, p. 161.

97. Richard Bridgman, *The Colloquial Style in America* (New York: Oxford University Press, 1968), p. 115.

98. Clemens, *Huck Finn*, p. 20.

99. Lubomir Doležel, *Narrative Modes in Czech Literature* (Toronto and Buffalo: University of Toronto Press, 1973), p. 42, fn. 37.

form of direct discourse. He makes no attempt to dissociate them from actual speech; they are not representative of "the nonverbal realm of consciousness."[100] In fact, when they are longer than a sentence or two, they take the form of debates; Huck poses his dilemma to himself and offers solutions. Early in the novel, Huck debates the topic of religion:

> I set down, one time, back in the woods, and had a long think about it. I says to myself, if a body can get anything they pray for, why don't Deacon Winn get back the money he lost on pork? Why can't the widow get back her silver snuff-box that was stole? Why can't Miss Watson fat up? No, says I to myself, there ain't nothing in it.[101]

When Huck decides to help the Wilks sisters get their money back from the King and Duke, he argues out his plan:

> I says to myself, shall I go to that doctor, private, and blow on these frauds? No—that won't do. He might tell who told him; then the king and the duke would make it warm for me. Shall I go, private, and tell Mary Jane? No—I dasn't do it. Her face would give them a hint, sure; they've got the money, and they'd slide right out and get away with it. If she was to fetch in help, I'd get mixed up in the business, before it was done with, I judge. No, there ain't no good way but one. I got to steal that money, somehow; and I got to steal it some way that they won't suspicion that I done it.[102]

On one occasion when Huck does use quotation marks to set off his thoughts, his dialogue, albeit a silent one, is with the King, not himself: "('House to rob, you *mean,*' says I to myself; 'and when you get through robbing it you'll come back here and wonder what's become of me and Jim and the raft—and you'll have to take it out in wondering.')"[103]

100. Cohn, *Transparent Minds,* p. 11.
101. Clemens, *Huck Finn,* pp. 14–15.
102. Ibid., p. 140.
103. Ibid., p. 166.

While the directly reported discourse in *Huck Finn* is both versatile and realistic, it occupies less space and is less significant than Huck's indirect representations. The novel's narration seems so much like direct discourse and the line between DD and ID is so blurred by Huck's reporting methods that the speaking voices spill over the quotation marks.

indirectly reported discourse

One of the great advantages Twain derives from Huck's apparent naïveté as a storyteller is Huck's casualness about the conventions of discourse reporting. His voice weaves in and out of those of other characters, leaving the discourse boundaries very fuzzy. As Huck says of his victuals, "things get mixed up, and the juice kind of swaps around, and the things go better."[104] Huck can move from narration (DN) to diffused indirectly reported discourse (ID) to direct discourse (DD) to compact ID in the course of one sentence:

> So Tom's Aunt Polly, she told all about who I was, and what; and I had to up and tell how I was in such a tight place that when Mrs. Phelps took me for Tom Sawyer— she chipped in and says, "Oh, go on and call me Aunt Sally, I'm used to it, now, and 'tain't no need to change"—that when Aunt Sally took me for Tom Sawyer, I had to stand it—there warn't no other way. . . .[105]

Because of this flexibility, indirect discourse is difficult to identify. Huck spends so much time telling the reader about what other people "say" that the accounts seem to be part of the story itself. It is interesting, though, that Twain is careful to make it seem as if Huck's ID does not serve one of its most typical narrative functions, that of summary. Huck cannot appear to condense conversations in the way that a more

104. Ibid., p. 7.
105. Ibid., p. 227.

sophisticated narrator does. Thus, when Huck recounts indirectly a charming conversation he and Jim have about "borrowing" food from the fields along the shore, Jim analyzes the various definitions of "borrowing" that Huck offers and Huck reports Jim's conclusions: "Jim said he reckoned the widow was partly right and pap was partly right. . . ."[106] Huck could easily have summarized here—"the widow and pap were both partly right"—but his method of reporting reflects both his lack of forethought (he just writes things down as they come) and his scrupulosity.

Huck's reports of other people's speech often involve words or phrases with which he is unfamiliar or which he would be unlikely to use. In reporting direct discourse, Huck misspells words alien to him or makes substitutions that may or may not be his own. The play on "deffersit" is one such example. Either Huck is unfamiliar with the word or he knows it but doesn't know how to spell it or he is spelling it to reflect the King and Duke's pronunciation. In the same episode, Huck repeatedly describes Peter Wilks as the "diseased" rather than the "deceased" when recounting the King's discourse, both direct and indirect. Since the King abuses many words, using "orgies" for "obsequies," for example, Huck may simply be quoting him; on the other hand, Huck himself may confuse "diseased/deceased." Occasionally, this play on spelling, and sometimes meaning, gets beyond Huck, as when the Duke says, while instructing the King in "the histrionic muse," " 'We want a little something to answer encores with, anyway.' " The King responds, " 'What's onkores, Bilgewater?' "[107] "Onkores" is eye-dialect and the misspelling only serves to identify the King's ignorance; his pronunciation is accurate. Huck is, no doubt, as unfamiliar with the word as the King, so it is Twain who has Huck spell it right the first time and wrong the second. Howells uses the same kind of

106. Ibid., p. 56.
107. Ibid., p. 110.

play on a French borrowing when Silas asks a question about the "Ongpeer" (the architect's "Empire") style, but the detached Howellsian narrator is competent to note this distinction, whereas Huck is not.

Huck's misspelling of some words is the only reflection of direct discourse in his indirect reports. When he says, "the king said the cubby would do for his valley—meaning me,"[108] we know Huck's account contains at least one word, "valley," attributable to the King. More significant are words that recur throughout the text, like "sivilize." Huck keeps his distance by misspelling the alien forms, and the reader recognizes them as someone else's words and sentiments. Occasionally Huck uses quotation marks to dissociate himself from a word, as when he tells the reader that Jim "said he must start in and 'terpret' it [his dream]."[109] Huck is mocking Jim in this scene and his punctuation may reflect a little condescension. Sometimes Huck will make a specific statement to attribute a word or phrase to another character. Thus he says, "After supper pap took the jug, and said he had enough whisky there for two drunks and one delirium tremens. That was always his word."[110] Finally, Huck might combine both quotation marks and a disclaimer for maximum distance: "Then they [the Duke and King] got tired of it, and allowed they would 'lay out a campaign,' as they called it."[111]

Some of Huck's compact ID resembles his unmarked direct discourse. As with UDD, a comma seems to signal the onset of another voice; however, the quoted (or semi-quoted) discourse contains a few ID features, putting it somewhere between UDD and compact ID: "Then he [Jim] studied it over and said, couldn't I put on some of them old things and dress up like a girl."[112] Aside from the fact that the question is not marked for Jim's dialect, it also contains the wrong verb tense

108. Ibid., p. 136.
109. Ibid., p. 71.
110. Ibid., p. 27.
111. Ibid., pp. 104–5.
112. Ibid., p. 47.

(*couldn't* for *can't*) and the wrong personal pronoun (*I* for you) for direct discourse.

Sometimes the onset of compact ID or semi-direct discourse is less obvious; often word choice, fragmentation, or emphasis identifies the fact that Huck has slipped into or out of another character's voice. Early in his story, Huck tells about a judge's ruling on his adoption: ". . . so he said courts mustn't interfere and separate families if they can help it; said he'd druther not take a child away from its father."[113] The portion preceding the semicolon sounds like direct quotation—Huck using the judge's words—but the *druther* seems to slip us back into Huck's voice. Huck goes on to report about the judge's attempts to reform Pap. How Huck got access to these dialogues and scenes is never explained—a bit of omniscience creeping in—although Huck does qualify one of his reports: "The judge said it was the holiest time on record, or something like that."[114] The final report is a mixture of Huck's and the judge's voices: "He [the judge] said he reckoned a body could reform the ole man with a shot-gun, maybe, but he didn't know no other way." The judge probably said "reform" and made reference to a shot-gun, but "ole" man and the double negative of the second clause belong to Huck.

Both fragmentation and emphasis mark the DD elements in some sentences. When he and Jim are reunited at the Grangerfords, Huck describes Jim's reaction: "He nearly cried, he was so glad, but he warn't surprised. Said he swum along behind me, that night, and heard me yell every time, but dasn't answer, because he didn't want nobody to pick *him* up, and take him into slavery again."[115] The same pattern—a description and then a fragment beginning with *said*—occurs in the following sentence: "The duke he grumbled; said the bag of gold was enough, and he didn't want to go no deeper—

113. Ibid., p. 22.
114. Ibid., p. 23.
115. Ibid., p. 92.

didn't want to rob a lot of orphans of *everything* they had."[116]
In some cases no *verbum dicendi* signals the shift, as when
Huck describes Mary Wilks's joy: ". . . she throws her arms
around my neck, and told me to say it *again,* say it *again,* say
it *again!*"[117] The emphasis and exclamation are Mary's, but
the explanation is Huck's. Sometimes merely a conversational
expression signals the mix of DD and ID: "The king said, *take
it all around,* it laid over any day he'd ever put in in the mission-
arying line. He said *it warn't no use talking,* heathens don't
amount to shucks, alongside of pirates, to work a campmeet-
ing with" (italics mine).[118]

Huck reports so much discourse indirectly that he has to
keep reminding the reader of the actual speaker. The place-
ment and form of Huck's tags indicate how faithful Huck is
to the original DD in his indirect reports. When he and Jim
are trapped on a wreck with a "gang of murderers" and must
hunt up a boat to escape, Huck reports: "Jim said he didn't
believe he could go any further—so scared he hadn't hardly
any strength left, he said."[119] The first part of the report, introduced by the *verbum dicendi,* "Jim said," seems more like
summary, although it retains a conversational verb construction, "didn't believe." The portion after the dash, with the
tag at the end, seems much closer to what Jim actually said,
with the fragmentary form, "so scared," and the double nega-
tives. Huck uses the same double tag in reporting a comment
of the Duke's: "So the duke said these Arkansaw lunkheads
couldn't come up to Shakespeare; what they wanted was low
comedy—and maybe something ruther worse than low comedy, he reckoned."[120] The second tag, "he reckoned," may be
merely a reminder of the reported speaker, but it has a special
significance here because Huck is presumably unaware of the

116. Ibid., p. 141.
117. Ibid., p. 148.
118. Ibid., p. 108.
119. Ibid., p. 60.
120. Ibid., p. 121.

Duke's intentions (he does not know what *low* means in this context) and, therefore, cannot be responsible for the innuendo of the clause preceding the tag.[121]

Critics of *Huck Finn* have used the direct/indirect discourse division to identify Huck's growth as a character and his involvement in the story. Although his explanation involves several overgeneralizations, Louis Rubin sums up this position clearly:

> In early episodes of the book, when Huck hears what is going on, he reports the news to us directly . . . But later, and especially in the episode in which Huck decides to go to Phelps Farm and steal Jim from captivity, Huck reports such matters indirectly. The way he relates and interprets is thus made part of his characterization . . . His personality thus deepens as the novel progresses, and the result is a much more ore profound exploration of the meaning of the experience Mark Twain is describing.[122]

Two of Huck's reports are most often cited as evidence for this hypothesis—his account of the King's "tears and flapdoodle" speech and his debate with his conscience in chapter 31. A number of critics have noted that Twain revised Huck's account of the King's speech from direct discourse in his original draft into indirect in the final draft to achieve greater irony in the presentation.[123] The single sentence presentation is,

---

121. Huck's sentences with tags after the main clause resemble in many ways a construction Tanya Reinhart labels "subject-oriented sentences containing parentheticals," such as, "He would be late, Ed said." Reinhart's parentheticals are tags like "Ed said" placed after the main clause. In the subject-oriented constructions the main clause reflects the point of view of its subject rather than of the speaker designated in the parenthetical (Tanya Reinhart, "Whose Main Clause? (Point of View in Sentences with Parentheticals)," *Harvard Studies in Syntax and Semantics,* ed. S. Kuno [Cambridge: Department of Linguistics, Harvard University, 1975] I: 143). See chapter 1, fn. 47.

122. Rubin, *Teller in the Tale,* p. 60.

123. Delancey Ferguson, *Mark Twain: Man and Legend* (New York: Russell & Russell, 1966), pp. 221–2; Smith, *Mark Twain,* p. 121.

in fact, only partially indirect; it subtly blends Huck's and the King's voices for maximum satiric effect.

HUCK	{ Well, by-and-by the king he gets up and comes forward a little, and works himself up and slobbers out a speech, all full of tears and flapdoodle about its being a sore trial
HUCK/ KING	{ for him and his poor brother to lose the diseased, and to miss seeing diseased alive, after the long journey of four
KING	{ thousand mile, but its a trial that's sweetened and sanctified to us by this dear sympathy and these holy tears, and
HUCK/ KING	{ so he thanks them out of his heart and out of his brother's heart, because out of their mouths they can't, words being
HUCK	{ too weak and cold, and all that kind of rot and slush, till it was just sickening; and then he blubbers out a pious goody-goody Amen, and turns himself loose and goes to crying fit to bust.[124]

Huck's narration frames his account of the King's speech. Twain begins with Huck's introduction, moves into Huck's rendition of the King's words ("its being a sore trial for him and his brother"), and finally, in the middle of the sentence, gives us the King himself speaking ("it's a trial that's sweetened and sanctified to us"). From this point on, we move gradually back to Huck's voice, passing once again through the intermediate stage of Huck's account of the King ("because out of their mouths they can't").

In reporting the speech indirectly, Huck takes on the satiric tone of the "moral man viewing an immoral society."[125] He could offer the same denunciation in an introduction or conclusion on a direct report, but since he is not given to "flat-footed" judgments, his opinions surface more subtly and more powerfully in the indirect presentation. The reader cannot enjoy the King's speech as a masterful con job because Huck's disgust subordinates the speech itself. As in the pas-

124. Clemens, *Huck Finn,* p. 169.
125. Smith, *Mark Twain,* p. 118.

sage in *Silas Lapham* on Silas' after-dinner talk, the narrator draws the reader into his condemnation by the distance he keeps from his character. More significantly, here the ironic relations of the novel shift as Huck allies himself with the author.

The satiric force of the passage hinges on the contrast between Huck's style and the bombastic posturings of the King. Huck's vocabulary in the frame clauses emphasizes his disdain. The King "slobbers," "blubbers," "works himself up," and "turns himself loose"; his speech, which Huck finds "sickening," is "rot," "slush," and "flapdoodle." When Huck actually records the King's speech, he adopts the King's ostentatiously pious vocabulary. The clichéd phrases, such as "sore trial," "poor brother," "sweetened and sanctified," and "holy tears," force the reader to focus on the pretense of genteel mourning. Tearfulness becomes a dominant theme, linking the paragraph to the surrounding descriptions where the King, the Duke, the Wilks sisters, and the townspeople carry on excessively. Huck's term "slush" effectively captures the mental and physical sogginess of the scene.

It is interesting to note that Twain shifts into the King's voice with a passive verb construction. Not only does the form obscure the change from third-person to first-person pronouns, it also adds a pompous note to the King's speech, contrasts the King's evasiveness to Huck's habitually straightforward style, and permits Twain to play on the repetition of "it's a trial," with its sermon-like rhythm.

The indirect discourse of this passage seems less contrived than Twain's attempts to integrate Huck's conscience's voice into his thought patterns. Yet, in both instances, Twain uses the form to gain an effect alien to Huck's personality. It is possible that we are seeing a growth in Huck's perceptual powers, but it is equally likely that, as Smith notes, ". . . Twain's satiric method requires that Huck be a mask for the writer, not a fully

126. Ibid.

developed character."[126] However, in at least one passage in the novel, Huck's use of indirect discourse reflects a deepening of his character totally consistent with his own experiences. During his climactic debate on his responsibility for Jim in chapter 31, Huck feels easy after he writes Miss Watson to turn Jim in, and he remembers the good fellowship that has passed between Jim and him. It is his simple, straightforward memories about their journey and, significantly, his memory of Jim's voice that prompt him to tear the letter up. Huck's love of the river and the process of drift, his attachment to Jim, and his instinctive, passive approach to life are all captured in the language of the passage.

> . . . and I see Jim before me, all the time, in the day, and in the night-time, sometimes moonlight, sometimes storms, and we a floating along, talking, and singing, and laughing. But somehow I couldn't seem to strike no places to harden me against him, but only the other kind. I'd see him standing my watch on top of his'n, stead of calling me, so I could go on sleeping; and see him how glad he was when I come back out of the fog; and when I come to him again in the swamp, up there where the feud was; and such-like times; and would always call me honey, and pet me, and do everything he could think of for me, and how good he always was; and at last I struck the time I saved him by telling the men we had small-pox aboard, and he was so grateful, and said I was the best friend old Jim ever had in the world, and the *only* one he's got now; and then I happened to look around, and see that paper.[127]

Huck's reflections synthesize the relationship between reader, narrator, and landscape. The memories Huck has are limited to experiences he has shared dramatically with Jim and the reader, and Huck's method of recording discourse introduces a significant ambiguity into this passage. When

127. Clemens, *Huck Finn*, p. 169.

Huck says of Jim "and said I was the best friend old Jim ever had in the world and the *only* one he's got now," the present-tense verb ("he's got") and the *now* suggest Huck is interpreting his relationship to Jim at the moment he is making his decision. However, the phrase seems to be embedded in what Jim said about events earlier in the novel. In fact, Huck is repeating almost verbatim Jim's earlier speech: " '. . . you's de bes' fren' Jim's ever had; en you's de *only* fren' ole Jim's got now.' "[128] If Huck's statement is a report of Jim's earlier discourse, then it is that rare fictional report which does, in fact, have a direct discourse antecedent.

But beyond the textual coherence Twain gains with it, the clause is significant for what it tells us about Huck. By distancing the clause from the tag, "[he] said," and by placing it in the present tense, Twain merges the past event with Huck's present dilemma. Jim is not present to make his case in person; it is Huck's memory of Jim and Jim's words that determines his change of heart. As Cox notes, "Huck has internalized the image of Jim."[129] Huck and Jim's voice have become one because Huck is not too particular about the way he records what he hears.

Huck Finn reveals a wide variety of reporting styles and many subtle uses of discourse. The technical facility Twain displays under the guise of Huck's naïveté demonstrates a sophistication at least equal to and in many ways surpassing his contemporaries. He creates irony, comedy, and a harmony among his characters by playing on Huck's presentation of his voice and the voices of the other characters. As in *Silas Lapham* and *The Bostonians,* the characters create themselves through their discourse, but in this novel, Huck also creates himself as a character through his narrative voice. Because the reader does not question Huck's sympathies, the ambiguities

128. Ibid., p. 74.
129. Cox, *Mark Twain*, p. 181.

in his reports are enriching rather than disturbing. They can distance him, as in his report of the King's speech, or bring him closer to another character as in his account of Jim. In many ways, the reader senses less authorial manipulation in the indirect discourse than in the direct. The fact that Huck is not too particular about his indirect reports results naturally from his characterization. That he should choose to report certain lengthy discourses directly seems less typical, and therefore indicates the author's control.

Huck Finn climaxes in chapter 31 when Huck decides to save Jim. Huck's rehearsal of his and Jim's journey is a lyrical summary of the central theme and events of the novel. But Twain created a dilemma, Jim's loss of freedom and separation from Huck, that he could not walk away from, and he chose to end the novel with a burlesque, a form he felt very comfortable with but which seems very "uncomfortable" for Huck. As character, Huck is overshadowed by Tom, and as narrator, Huck seems to lose control of his story. His descriptions become strained and his accounts of other characters, while technically interesting, seem less significant to the progress of the story. For example, a frenzied quality invades Huck's description of Tom's escape plan. When Aunt Sally notes that one of Uncle Silas' shirts is missing, Huck describes his momentary panic:

> My heart fell down amongst my lungs and livers and things, and a hard piece of corn-crust started down my throat after it and got met on the road with a cough and was shot across the table and took one of the children in the eye and curled him up like a fishing-worm, and let a cry out of him the size of a war-whoop and Tom he turned kinder blue around the gills, and it amounted to a considerable state of things for about a quarter of a minute or as much as that, and I would a sold out for half price if there was a bidder. But after that we was all right again—it was the sudden surprise of it that knocked us so kind of cold.[130]

130. Clemens, *Huck Finn*, p. 198.

The events described in this passage happen haphazardly, seemingly beyond Huck's control. If we compare the structure of this sentence to one in which Huck describes activities within his control, such as in his account of his escape from Pap, the differences are obvious. Huck's earlier description moves along with compound predicates, but a number of syntactic variations control the pace. He estimates the quantity of rocks with the qualification, "all I could drag"; he carefully provides the reader with a sense of direction and location by using the prepositional phrases "through the woods" and "down to the river"; and he uses juxtaposition to create a marked rhythm in the final clause "down it sunk, out of sight." By contrast, in this passage, Huck throws together his and Tom's reaction to the entire state of affairs in one run-on sentence that lacks even the implication of subordination. No significant repetitions bind the sentence together thematically. The sentence's frantic pace seems out of proportion to the amount of real danger that Huck and Tom face, and the exaggeration results in a near parody of Huck's style. Huck is a part of the ridiculous scene, and his style is a reflection of his complicity.

In scenes preceding the conclusion, Twain gradually reduces the distance between himself and Huck and between Huck and the reader. Huck's account of the King's speech and his moving tribute to Jim reflect his maturation as narrator and character. As I noted above, some critics read Huck's introduction to the Phelps farm as a record of Twain's own despair, thus suggesting the degree to which Twain's and Huck's perspectives have merged. The "implied" author has come closer to his narrator/protagonist just as James's and Howells' narrators grew closer to their main characters. It would have been difficult at this point for Twain to reestablish the ironic distance from Huck that he maintained in the first portion of the novel. Twain chooses, therefore, to have Huck immerse himself in his own story and become an uncritical participant and observer. This solution, like the ones James and Howells developed to solve their "narrator" problems, creates complications for characterization. The reader is left with some unanswered questions about Huck. He excites our admiration with his thoughtful commitment to Jim and then unthinkingly prolongs Jim's captivity by his childish allegiance to Tom. Like Howells, Twain pulls back from his character just when he has portrayed him most sympathetically.

In *Huck Finn* Twain proved the potential of the colloquial style of narration. He found in the naïve narrator both a legitimate and an unobtrusive narrative voice, one that could mingle freely with the voices of other characters. But Huck's very naïveté created a dilemma for Twain's realistic technique. Having eliminated the external authority and perspective and having created a supremely subjective narrative, he was forced to reimpose order on his story in order to bring it to a close.

Nevertheless, the unique potential of Huck's colloquial narration haunted future generations of American novelists. Twain himself never again used Huck's innovative voice effectively. Thus, for example, in "Tom Sawyer Abroad" (1894) and "Tom Sawyer, Detective" (1896), Huck narrates but Tom is the center of attention. Other narrators, Hank Morgan, for instance, in *A Connecticut Yankee in King Arthur's Court* (1889), did not limit Twain enough. Only in the *Autobiography* where he was not compelled to maintain a consistent narrative persona, does he approximate his achievement in *Huck Finn,* but there his purpose was so loose that it provided no focus for the style. In *Huck Finn* he proved the potential of the colloquial style of narration. His challenge to traditional forms of literary discourse is one of American realism's lasting legacies to the novel.

5
the
american
realists
and
their
legacy

Despite the differences in subject matter and cultural orientation, a clear pattern, involving methods of presentation, emerges in these three novels to link the authors and to demonstrate the very important contributions they made collectively to the form of the American novel. If we consider narration in terms of the relationship among author, narrator, character, and reader, we can see each of these authors attempting to confront the reader more directly with the characters by aligning the narrator's perspective with those of the characters and, at times, distancing the narrator from the "implied" author. Responsibility for the interpretation of the story shifts away from the narrator and toward the reader.

Thus, these writers rejected the omniscient narrator, a narrative voice that represents the sensibilities of the "implied" author, that is authoritative, and that guides the reader through the novel. Such a narrator shares with the reader a distance from characters and events that enables the reader to accept his judgments as definitive. In good fiction employing this narrative mode, the reader does not feel patronized or railroaded; in fact, he marvels at the author's skill in convincing and enlightening him. The realists were, however, acutely aware of the degree to which the omniscient narrator distances the reader from the fiction itself—how, particularly in its less skillful manifestations, the form emphasizes the fictitiousness of the novel. They saw this fairy-tale quality of "make believe" as realism's greatest enemy, and their work demonstrates their efforts to counteract its effects.

It was in the manner of telling their stories, as much as in the subject matter itself, that they sought to create the illusion of life, to attest to the honesty and authenticity of their fiction. For James it was the "direct impression of life"; for Twain it was "homely wisdom and rugged honesty"; for Howells "realism is nothing more and nothing less than the truthful treatment of materials."[1] Their commitment to honesty and truthfulness, to the human limitations of the storyteller, depended on cultural as well as on literary considerations. Henry Nash Smith's evaluation of Twain can be extended to all three writers: "Thus his technical innovations might be described with equal accuracy as an ethical, a sociological, or a literary undertaking."[2] The uncertainties of the post–Civil War era, the upheavals of industrialization, the dissolution of the pastoral myth made these writers question the arrogance of the "all-knowing" voice. It was more important to confront the reader with life's uncertainties without offering easy explanations than to lull him into a false sense of security with neatly interpreted romantic tales.

---

1. Quoted by Warner Berthoff in *The Ferment of Realism: American Literature, 1884–1919* (New York: The Free Press, 1965) from James's "Deerfield Letter" on the page of epigrams preceding Berthoff's page 1; Henry Nash Smith, *Mark Twain: The Development of a Writer* (New York: Atheneum, 1967), p. 4; quoted in "Realism Defined: William Dean Howells," *Literary History of the United States: History*, ed. R. E. Spiller, *et al.*, 4th ed., rev. (New York: Macmillan, 1974), p. 879.

2. Smith, *Mark Twain*, p. vii.

Their theory of fiction led the realists to attack vigorously and directly the problem of how to shape a new role for the narrator in fiction. Each of them developed a slightly different solution, but their basic approach was, perhaps inevitably, the same: if the narrator is to be less prominent, then the discourse of the characters must become more so. The inverse proportion of this relationship is crucial to the realists' technique. These novelists were not the first in the American tradition to write good dialogue nor were they the first to experiment with forms of indirect discourse, but never before in our fiction had discourse been so crucial to the telling of the tale. For the realists, dialogue is not a frill or a filler to break up the narrator's exposition; it is in itself a key to exposition and characterization.

The realists discovered an important linguistic principle long before linguists began to consider the issue: namely, responsibility for directly reported discourse belongs to the speaker alone. Through direct discourse, the characters can come to the reader without mediation. The fact that the author creates the discourse just as he creates the characters is one of the paradoxes of realism. But the realists' faith in the expressive powers of language helped them to confront the paradox. That characters should talk and act like "real" people and that the writer is responsible to see that they do is yet another plank in the realists' doctrine. The link between characterization and expression is nowhere more emphatically stated than in Twain's list of "Fenimore Cooper's Literary Offenses." On the discourse of characters, Twain says:

> They [the rules] require that when the personages of a tale deal in conversation, the talk shall sound like human talk, and be talk such as human beings would be likely to talk in the given circumstances, and have a discoverable meaning, also a discoverable purpose, and a show of relevancy, and remain in the neighborhood of the subject in hand, and be interesting to the reader, and help out the

tale, and stop when the people cannot think of anything
more to say.[3]

James, Howells, and Twain made an art of dialogue, an art
amply demonstrated in the analyses in preceding chapters.
Their interest in shaping dialogue to sound like "real" talk,
like their concern for narrative perspective, was rooted in ide-
ology. Listening to the voices of "common" people in ordinary conversations and rendering those voices faithfully and
realistically represents an "egalitarian faith"[4] in the value of
the individual. Moreover, the realists were preoccupied with
characterization and the presentation of the individual, subjective reality. It is only through the representation of many
voices and many perspectives that an objective reality
emerges. As Terrence Doody notes, ". . . realism achieves its
objectivity by recognizing the inviolable subjectivity of all its
human characters, the potential equal value and authority of
every individual, the possibility of another point of view."[5]
The prominence realists gave to characters' voices and perspectives and the care they took to represent the individuality
of those voices offers a striking contrast to fiction of the romantic tradition. Through Ishmael, Melville tells us in a passage in *Moby-Dick* that in order to portray "man, in the
ideal,"[6] he must attribute to characters certain qualities, and
by extension speech traits, that are quite unexpected:

> If, then, to meanest mariners, renegades and castaways,
> I shall hereafter ascribe high qualities, though dark;
> weave round them tragic graces; if even the most mourn-

3. Samuel Langhorne Clemens, in *Literary Essays*, vol. 22 of *The Writings of Mark Twain*, Author's National Edition (New York: Harper & Brothers, 1918), p. 61.

4. Leo Marx, "The Vernacular Tradition in American Literature," in *Studies in American Culture*, ed. Joseph J. Kwiat and Mary C. Turpie (Minneapolis: University of Minnesota Press, 1960), p. 113.

5. Terrence Doody, *"Don Quixote, Ulysses, and the Idea of Realism," Novel* 12 (1979), p. 201.

6. Herman Melville, *Moby-Dick*, ed. Harrison Hayford and Hershel Parker (New York: W. W. Norton & Company, Inc., 1967), p. 69.

ful, perchance the most abased, among them all, shall at
times lift himself to the exalted mounts . . . then against
all mortal critics bear me out in it, thou just Spirit of
Equality, which hast spread one royal mantle of humanity
over all my kind![7]

The romantics and the realists share the same faith in the
power of language, but for the realist, language expresses life;
for the romantic, it interprets it. Despite the fact that on occasion "among his lesser characters Melville displayed considerable versatility in composing dialogue,"[8] his focus was on
the universal, not on the particular.

James, Howells, and Twain all dabbled in the theater and
took themselves quite seriously as playwrights. Their failure
in this medium is, in a sense, a telling commentary on their
success as storytellers. In fiction, conversation must be, as
James's mild criticism of Howells asserts, ". . . distributed, interspaced with narrative and pictorial matter."[9] The narrator
must be unobtrusive, but he must remain. One way to assert
the narrator's presence without insisting on it is to give him
the freedom to condense and to filter discourse by representing it indirectly. The realists do not take indirect reporting
for granted by assuming the narrator's right to usurp the
character's responsibility in the report. Rather, these writers
were reaching for a new variety of indirect discourse—one
that remains true to the character's perspective while simultaneously offering narrator comment. They also developed a
new role for this discourse form. The interpretation of key
scenes and events in their novels often hinges upon the representation of the character's perception. The realists' indirect
discourse demonstrates a sympathy for characters that shades

7. Melville, *Moby-Dick*, pp. 104–5.
8. Richard Bridgman, *The Colloquial Style in America* (New York: Oxford University Press, 1968), p. 69.
9. Henry James, "William Dean Howells," rpt. in *Howells: A Century of Criticism*, ed. Kenneth E. Eble (Dallas: Southern Methodist University Press, 1967), p. 50.

into ambiguity, and it minimizes the ironic edge that such indirect reports can create. Even where no ambiguity exists, the sympathy the discourse generates softens ironic distance. We may feel disdain for Silas at the Corey dinner, but we also feel pain.

The novels in this study represent a concerted and daring experimentation with new techniques of storytelling—experimentation that American realists shared with many of their European contemporaries. The narration of these novels indicates a true uneasiness with the traditional narrator and an equally intense unwillingness to relinquish the author/narrator's prerogative to guide the reader. Characters' discourse comes to share the stage with the narrator's voice, but it does not supplant it. This tension between "telling" and "showing" results in the less than satisfactory endings of each of these novels, but issues other than methodology contribute to the problem endings. Uneasy as these writers were with authority, they were committed to it, and their commitment was, in fact, a moral one, rooted in their conception of realism.

The realists were intent on presenting the complexity of life in order that readers might recognize in it their own humanity and come to terms with it. Howells offers a very clear articulation of this responsibility:

> . . . the business of the novelist is to make you understand the real world through his faithful effigy of it; . . . to arrange a perspective for you with everything in its proper relation and proportion to everything else, and this so manifest that you cannot err in it however myopic or astigmatic you may be. It is his function to help you to be kinder, juster to yourself, truer to all.[10]

Even James, who was more comfortable with ambiguity and less given to didacticism, insisted on the need to represent

10. William Dean Howells, "Novel-Writing and Novel-Reading: An Impersonal Explanation," ed. William M. Gibson in *Howells and James: A Double Billing* (New York: The New York Public Library, 1958), p. 24.

complexity in order that the reader might perceive and appreciate life more fully. The narrator might become less authoritative, but the overall presentation must demonstrate the moral responsibility the realists felt so keenly.

The dilemma the realists faced—the tension between technique and morality—became more, not less, intense for their immediate successors. In the fiction of Crane, Dreiser, and Anderson we see an increasing emphasis on characters' self-expression, through the representation of their speech and thought. At the same time, however, the narrator becomes more, not less, distanced from the characters. Characters are types to be scrutinized, studied, and ultimately judged in terms of the social conditions that produce them. Juxtaposed against his authentic dialogue, which often captures the inarticulateness of his characters, is Stephen Crane's narrative voice, which dwells on the often grotesque physical details of characters and setting and refers to characters as "the urchin" and "the babe." An excerpt from *Maggie: A Girl of the Streets* demonstrates the distance between narrator and characters:

> As the sullen-eyed man, followed by the blood-covered boy, drew near, the little girl burst into reproachful cries. "Ah, Jimmie, youse bin fightin' agin."
> The urchin swelled disdainfully.
> "Ah, what d'hell, Mag. See?"
> The little girl upbraided him. "Youse allus fightin', Jimmie, an' yeh knows it puts mudder out when yehs come home half dead, an' it's like we'll all get a poundin'."
> She began to weep. The babe threw back his head and roared at his prospects.[11]

The narrator does not comment on the squalor, the pitifulness, of this scene; his detachment is almost clinical. However, his observations—"the sullen-eyed man," "the blood-

11. Stephen Crane, *Maggie: A Girl of the Streets*, in *Great Short Works of Stephen Crane*, intro. by James B. Colvert (New York: Harper & Row, 1968), p. 131.

covered boy"—are not tentative, and they are heavy with implications that the reader cannot escape. At the same time,
the very authenticity of the dialogue distances the reader from
the characters, because it is so difficult to read.

In *An American Tragedy*, Dreiser offers an extensive representation of Clyde Griffith's thoughts and feelings by using
a wide variety of discourse types, but his remarkable skill with
these forms is often overshadowed by his narrator's clumsy
philosophizing.

> There are moments when in connection with the sensi-
> tively imaginative or morbidly anachronistic—the mental-
> ity assailed and the same not of any great strength and
> the problem confronting it of sufficient force and com-
> plexity—the reason not actually toppling from its throne,
> still totters or is warped or shaken—the mind befuddled
> to the extent that for the time being, at least, unreason
> or disorder and mistaken or erroneous counsel would ap-
> pear to hold against all else.[12]

Here, the narrator's rhetoric, rather than the absence of commentary, distances him from his character, but his voice actually competes with Clyde's in the novel. No longer content
with psycho-narration, mere summaries of thought, Dreiser
shows us his character thinking. In the climactic scenes of the
novel, we hear Clyde's evil impulses address him directly, like
Huck's conscience, and we hear Clyde's internal voice, as free
indirect discourse, offer both parenthetical and direct commentary on events: "(Would that train never get here?)"; "(If
only his knees and hands wouldn't tremble so at times.)";
"So this was the end of all that wonderful dream. And for this
he had sought so desperately to disengage himself from Ro-
berta—even to the point of deciding to slay her."[13] Dreiser's
rendering of discourse clearly demonstrates ". . . James's final

---

12. Theodore Dreiser, *An American Tragedy,* afterword by Irving Howe (New York:
The New American Library, 1964), p. 463.
13. Ibid., pp. 474, 474, and 790.

artistic faith in the drama of the mind,"[14] and it creates a bond between character and reader that his narrator's voice often interrupts.

The writers of the post-realistic period worked toward depersonalizing the narrator; in the majority of their fiction, they removed the narrating "I" that the realists had retained. To a lesser extent, in the stories of Ring Lardner and Sherwood Anderson, for example, they experimented with the highly subjective, naïve narrator modeled after Huck Finn. In both approaches the narrator tends to stand apart from his story; at the same time, the characters' speech and thought become even more prominent than in the realists' fiction. Yet, controlling perspective within the story continued to be a problem.

It remained for the great writers of the modernist period to capitalize fully on the realists' technical discoveries. Their success must be attributed in part to their willingness to forego the right to judge, to trust the reader to his own devices, and to relinquish, at least apparently, the responsibility of arranging "everything in its proper relation and proportion to everything else," as Howells said. Readers must draw their own conclusions from modern fiction on the basis of what characters think and say, and characters become defiantly individual. On the one hand, we have Hemingway's short stories that tell themselves in dialogue, the interpolating voice of the narrator being almost completely absent. Dialogue is not superfluous; it is all. On the other hand, we have Faulkner's representation of "stream of consciousness" in which the characters' thoughts and feelings seem to come to us directly. Again, the narrator has disappeared. Douglas Hewitt summarizes the form: "Thus we come close to the 'impersonal novel' (I adopt the term from Wayne Booth) to the conception of the novel not as like the experience of hearing about life from someone we trust but as like life itself."[15]

14. Gordon O. Taylor, *The Passages of Thought: Psychological Representation in the American Novel, 1870–1900* (New York: Oxford University Press, 1969), p. 157.

For many modern writers, the expression of consciousness, the representation of perspective, becomes an end in itself. This interest translates into a "preoccupation with the medium," as Charles Feidelson notes.[16] Modern writers push their medium, language, and their form, the novel, to the limit to accommodate the new demands of characterization, and they require sophisticated and participatory readers. The narrator ceases to mediate between the character and the reader's experience of him, between the reader and the text. The realists opened the door to this "impersonal" mode by limiting the narrator's control and by foregrounding the voices of characters. Their concern for the authenticity of characterization also contributed to these technical innovations. Twain had to find a way to let his "outlaw" talk in a respectable frame; James had to find a means of articulating an obsessed woman's consciousness; Howells had to give his sympathy for Silas expression in the text. In addition, however, the realists opened the possibility of irresponsible and unreliable presentations, for when characters speak for themselves, we are not always sure of their limitations. Thus, as Hewitt says:

> The result, in short, of the novelist's claimed withdrawal from his novel—a withdrawal which, it has often been asserted, permits a more direct presentation of the world without the interposition of a narrator—is often to oblige us to read the word in an extremely sophisticated way as an objective correlative for a vision which may leave us in grave doubts as to its trustworthiness.[17]

The realists' own reluctance to leave these doubts (of the three, James was the most willing to trust the reader), is evident in their uneasiness about effacing the narrator.

15. Douglas Hewitt, *The Approach to Fiction: Good and Bad Readings of Novels* (London: Longman, 1972), p. 70.

16. Charles Feidelson Jr., *Symbolism and American Literature* (Chicago: The University of Chicago Press, 1963), p. 45.

17. Hewitt, *Approach to Fiction*, p. 83.

We return, then, full circle to the question, addressed in the introduction, of what constitutes a narrative mode and of how narration combines with characters' discourse to create a novel. We have in modern fiction, what Chatman calls " 'non'—or minimally narrated"[18] stories. The narrator's voice all but disappears to be replaced by the voices of characters. When characters speak to the reader directly, either in direct discourse or in what Cohn labels "autonomous monologue" ("that singular narrative genre entirely constituted by a fictional character's thoughts"), we recognize "the absence of a manipulating narrator."[19] The story is still "authored," but the evidence of that control in the language of the text is minimal or nonexistent.

Narration does not depend solely on the fact that information is present in a story that no character can know, as Banfield, *et al.*, would have us believe; rather, narration depends on language. Language of the text other than the direct discourse of the characters is always at least partially the responsibility of the narrator, no matter how effaced or distanced he may be. Only when a text is composed entirely of direct discourse, whether marked or unmarked, can it be called "narratorless," but there are gradations between the most covert and overt of narrators. The realists tried to strike a balance by minimizing the narrator's authority. Thus, the narrator can be distinguished as fully as possible from the author; he can refuse to offer judgments; or his voice can be supplanted by the voices of characters. Ultimately, the voices in the language of the novel explain the narrator's role.

A close examination of the realists' technique demonstrates the inadequacy of much of our current discussion of narration. In order to understand the realists' attempts to foreground the perspectives of their characters, we must be able

18. Seymour Chatman, *Story and Discourse: Narrative Structure of Fiction and Film* (Ithaca and London: Cornell University Press, 1978), p. 196.

19. Dorrit Cohn, *Transparent Minds: Narrative Modes for Presenting Consciousness in Fiction* (Princeton: Princeton University Press, 1978), pp. 218 and 219.

to sort out linguistic responsibility in the text. The relationship between narration and discourse is a continuum with frequent overlaps. Narration is not a fixed commodity; rather it engages in a dynamic interaction with the discourse elements of the novel. These discourse types are not fixed and easily classifiable; they shade into one another, creating endless ambiguity, which can sometimes be sorted out in context and sometimes remains. The successful novelist exploits this relationship to enrich his reader's experience with the text.

list of works cited

prefatory note

I have found several studies particularly helpful for the organization and presentation of my analyses. Doležel and Chatman synthesize and expand many insights of structuralist/formalist criticism and apply their formulations to the analysis of the language of fiction. They take into account both the narrator's and the characters' discourse. Several relevant works are not specifically cited in the text of this study: Roy Pascal, *The Dual Voice: Free Indirect Speech and Its Functioning in the Nineteenth-Century European Novel* (Totowa, New Jersey: Rowman and Littlefield, 1977); W. J. M. Bronzwaer, *Tense in the Novel: An Investigation of Some Potentialities of Linguistic Criticism* (Gröningen: Wolters-Noordhoff Publishing, 1970); Mikhail Bakhtin, *Problems of Dostoevsky's Poetics,* trans. R. W. Rotsel (Ann Arbor, Mich.: Ardis, 1973). Norman Page's *Speech in the English Novel* (London: Longman, 1973) looks only at characters' discourse, but his model is well formulated and useful for analysis. Volume 2 (No. 2, Winter, 1981) of *Poetics Today* has a number of interesting essays on narration and on characters' discourse and discourse types.

a. approaches to narration and discourse

Banfield, Ann. "Narrative Style and the Grammar of Direct and Indirect Speech," *Foundations of Language* 10 (1973), 1–39.
_____. "The Formal Coherence of Represented Speech and Thought," *Poetics and Theory of Literature* 3 (1978), 289–314.

Booth, Wayne. *The Rhetoric of Fiction.* Chicago: University of Chicago Press, 1961.

Chatman, Seymour. *Story and Discourse: Narrative Structure of Fiction and Film.* Ithaca and London: Cornell University Press, 1978.

Cohn, Dorrit. *Transparent Minds: Narrative Modes for Presenting Consciousness in Fiction.* Princeton: Princeton University Press, 1978.

Dillon, George and Frederick Kirchhoff. "On the Form and Function of Free Indirect Style," *Poetics and Theory of Literature* 1 (1976), 431–40.

Doležel, Lubomir. *Narrative Modes in Czech Literature.* Toronto and Buffalo: University of Toronto Press, 1973.

Fillmore, Charles. "Pragmatics and the Description of Discourse," *Berkeley Studies in Syntax and Semantics.* C. Fillmore, G. Lakoff, R. Lakoff, eds. Berkeley: Department of Linguistics and Institute for Human Learning, University of California, 1 (1974), V-1–V-21.

Friedman, Norman. *Form and Meaning in Fiction.* Athens: The University of Georgia Press, 1975.

Genette, Gérard. *Figures III.* Paris: Seuil, 1972.

Green, Georgia. "Main Clause Phenomena in Subordinate Clauses," *Language* 52 (1976), 382–97.

Hamburger, Käte. *The Logic of Literature,* trans. Marilynn J. Ross. Bloomington and London: Indiana University Press, 1973.

Hernadi, Paul. *Beyond Genre: New Directions in Literary Classification.* Ithaca and London: Cornell University Press, 1972.

Joos, Martin. *The English Verb: Form & Meanings.* Madison: University of Wisconsin Press, 1968.

Kuroda, S.-Y. "Reflections on the Foundations of Narrative Theory: From a Linguistic Point of View," in *Pragmatics of Language and Literature.* Teun A. van Dijk, ed. Amsterdam: North-Holland Publishing Company, 1976, pp. 107–40.

————. "Where Epistemology, Style, and Grammar Meet: A Case Study from Japanese," in *A Festschrift for Morris Halle.* Stephen R. Anderson and Paul Kiparsky, eds. New York: Holt, Rinehart & Winston, 1973, pp. 377–91.

Lakoff, Robin. "Language in Context," *Language* 48 (1972), 907–27.

McHale, Brian. "Free Indirect Discourse: A Survey of Recent Accounts," *Poetics and Theory of Literature* 3 (1978), 249–87.

Ohmann, Richard. "Generative Grammars and the Concept of Literature," *Word* 20 (1964), 423–39.

Partee, Barbara Hall. "The Syntax and Semantics of Quotation," in *A Festschrift for Morris Halle*. Stephen R. Anderson and Paul Kiparsky, eds. New York: Holt, Rinehart & Winston, 1973, pp. 412–30.

Reinhart, Tanya. "Whose Main Clause? (Point of View in Sentences with Parentheticals)," *Harvard Studies in Syntax and Semantics*. S. Kuno, ed. Cambridge: Department of Linguistics, Harvard University, 1 (1975), 127–71.

Romberg, Bertil. *Studies in the Narrative Technique of the First-Person Novel*. Lund, Sweden: Almqvist & Wiksell, 1962.

Ross, Donald, Jr. "Who's Talking? How Characters become Narrators in Fiction," *Modern Language Notes* 91 (1976), 1222–42.

Ross, John Robert, "On Declarative Sentences," in *Readings in English Transformational Grammar*. R. A. Jacobs and P.S. Rosenbaum, eds. Waltham, Mass.: Ginn, 1970, pp. 222–72.

Stanzel, Franz. *Narrative Situations in the Novel: Tom Jones, Moby-Dick, The Ambassadors, Ulysses*, trans. James P. Pusack. Bloomington: Indiana University Press, 1971.

——————. "Second Thoughts on *Narrative Situations in the Novel*: Towards a " 'Grammar of Fiction,' " *Novel* 11 (1978), 247–64.

Uspensky, Boris. *A Poetics of Composition: The Structure of the Artistic Text and Typology of a Compositional Form*, trans. V. Zavarin and S. Wittig. Berkeley and Los Angeles: University of California Press, 1973.

b. american realistic fiction: texts and criticism

Beach, Joseph Warren. *The Method of Henry James*. New Haven: Yale University Press, 1918.

Berthoff, Warner. *The Ferment of Realism: American Literature, 1884–1919*. New York: The Free Press, 1965.

Blair, Walter. *Mark Twain & Huck Finn*. Berkeley and Los Angeles: University of California Press, 1960.

——————. "When was *Huckleberry Finn* Written?" *American Literature* 30 (1958), 1–25.

Boggan, J. R. "That Slap, Huck, Did It Hurt?" *English Language Notes* 1 (March, 1964), 212–15.

Branch, Edgar Marquess. *The Literary Apprenticeship of Mark Twain, with Selections from His Apprentice Writing*. New York: Russell & Russell, 1966.

Bridgman, Richard. *The Colloquial Style in America.* New York: Oxford University Press, 1968.

Brown, Marshall. "The Logic of Realism: A Hegelian Approach," *PMLA* 96 (1981), 224–41.

Cady, Edwin H. *The Light of Common Day: Realism in American Fiction.* Bloomington and London: Indiana University Press, 1971.

Canby, Henry Seidel. *Turn West, Turn East: Mark Twain and Henry James.* New York: Biblo and Tannen, 1965.

Cargill, Oscar. *The Novels of Henry James.* New York: Hefner Publishing Company, 1971.

Carrington, George C., Jr. *The Dramatic Unity of "Huckleberry Finn."* Columbus: Ohio State University Press, 1976.

_____. *The Immense Complex Drama: The World and Art of the Howells Novel.* Columbus: Ohio State University Press, 1966.

Clemens, Samuel Langhorne. "A Complaint about Correspondents," in *The Celebrated Jumping Frog of Calaveras County and Other Sketches.* 1867; rpt. Upper Saddle River, N.J.: Literature House, 1969, pp. 26–33.

_____. *Adventures of Huckleberry Finn: An Authoritative Text, Backgrounds and Sources, Criticism.* Sculley Bradley, Richmond Croom Beatty, E. Hudson Long, Thomas Cooley, eds. New York: W. W. Norton & Company, Inc., 1977.

_____. "Cooper's Prose Style," in *Letters from the Earth.* Bernard DeVoto, ed. New York: Harper & Row, 1962, pp. 117–24.

_____. "Fenimore Cooper's Literary Offenses," in *Literary Essays,* Vol. 22 of *The Writings of Mark Twain,* Author's National Edition. New York: Harper & Brothers, 1918, pp. 60–77.

_____. "Letter to Andrew Lang 1890 (?)" in *Mark Twain: The Critical Heritage.* Frederick Anderson, ed. London: Routledge & Kegan Paul, 1971, pp. 334–36.

_____. *Mark Twain's Autobiography.* Albert Bigelow Paine, ed., 2 vols. New York: Harper & Brothers, 1924.

_____. *Mark Twain's Letters.* Albert Bigelow Paine, ed., 2 vols. New York: Harper & Brothers, 1917.

_____. "My Methods of Writing," *Mark Twain Quarterly* 8 (Winter–Spring, 1949), 1.

_____. "William Dean Howells," rpt. in *Howells: A Century of Criticism.* Kenneth E. Eble, ed. Dallas: Southern Methodist University Press, 1962, pp. 78–87.

Clerc, Charles. "Sunrise on the River: 'The Whole World' of Huckleberry Finn," *Modern Fiction Studies* 14 (Spring, 1968), 67–78.

Covici, Pascal, Jr. *Mark Twain's Humor: The Image of a World.* Dallas: Southern Methodist University Press, 1962.

Cox, James. *Mark Twain: The Fate of Humor.* Princeton: Princeton University Press, 1966.

Crane, Stephen. *Great Short Works of Stephen Crane.* Intro. by James B. Colvert. New York: Harper & Row, 1968.

Doody, Terrence. *"Don Quixote, Ulysses,* and the Idea of Realism," *Novel* 12 (1979), 197–214.

Dreiser, Theodore. *An American Tragedy.* Afterword by Irving Howe. New York: New American Library, 1964.

Emerson, Ralph Waldo. *The Selected Writings of Ralph Waldo Emerson.* Brooks Atkinson, ed. New York: Random House, 1950.

Feidelson, Charles, Jr. *Symbolism and American Literature.* Chicago: The University of Chicago Press, 1963.

Ferguson, Delancey. *Mark Twain: Man and Legend.* New York: Russell & Russell, 1966.

Gerber, John C. "Mark Twain's Use of the Comic Pose," *PMLA* 77 (1962), 297–304.

_____. "The Relation between Point of View and Style in the Works of Mark Twain," in *Style in Prose Fiction: English Institute Essays, 1958.* Ed. with foreword by Harold C. Martin. New York: Columbia University Press, 1959, pp. 142–71.

Gibson, William M. *The Art of Mark Twain.* New York: Oxford University Press, 1976.

Habegger, Alfred. "The Disunity of *The Bostonians,"* *Nineteenth-Century Fiction* 24 (1969), 193–209.

Hewitt, Douglas. *The Approach to Fiction: Good and Bad Readings of Novels.* London: Longman, 1972.

Howard, David. *"The Bostonians,"* in *The Air of Reality: New Essays on Henry James.* John Goode, ed. London: Metheun & Co., Ltd., 1972, pp. 60–80.

Howells, William Dean. "Henry James, Jr.," rpt. in *W. D. Howells as Critic.* Edwin H. Cady, ed. London and Boston: Routledge & Kegan Paul, 1973.

_____. *My Mark Twain: Reminiscences and Criticisms.* Ed. with intro. by Marilyn Austin Baldwin. Baton Rouge: Louisiana State University Press, 1967.

—————. "Novel-Writing and Novel-Reading: An Impersonal Explanation," in *Howells and James: A Double Billing.* William M. Gibson, ed. New York: The New York Public Library, 1958.

—————. "On Truth in Fiction," rpt. in *Documents of Modern Literary Realism.* George J. Becker, ed. Princeton: Princeton University Press, 1963, pp. 129–36.

—————. *The Rise of Silas Lapham.* Intro. and notes to the Text by Walter J. Meserve, Text established by Walter J. Meserve and David J. Nordloh. Bloomington and London: Indiana University Press, 1971.

Jakobson, Roman. "On Realism in Art," in *Readings in Russian Poetics: Formalist and Structuralist Views.* Ladislav Matejka and Krystyna Pomorska, eds. Ann Arbor: Michigan Slavic Publications, 1978, pp. 38–46.

—————. "Two Aspects of Language and Two Types of Aphasic Disturbances," in *Fundamentals of Language.* R. Jakobson and Morris Halle, eds. The Hague: Mouton & Co., 1956, pp. 55–82.

James, Henry. "The Art of Fiction," in *The Portable Henry James.* Ed. and with an intro. by Morton Dauwen Zabel, rev. by Lyall H. P. Powers. New York: The Viking Press, 1968.

—————. *The Art of the Novel: Critical Prefaces.* Intro. by Richard P. Blackmur. New York: Charles Scribner's Sons, 1962.

—————. *The Bostonians.* Ed. with intro. by Irving Howe. New York: The Modern Library, Random House, 1956.

—————. *The Letters of Henry James.* Selected and ed. by Percy Lubbock. New York: Octagon Books, 1948; rpt. 1970.

—————. "William Dean Howells," rpt. in *Howells: A Century of Criticism.* Kenneth E. Eble, ed. Dallas: Southern Methodist University Press, 1962.

Kaplan, Justin. *Mr. Clemens and Mark Twain: A Biography.* New York: Simon and Schuster, 1966.

Kolb, Harold, Jr. *The Illusion of Life: American Realism as a Literary Form.* Charlottesville: The University Press of Virginia, 1969.

Krause, Sydney J. "Twain's Method and Theory of Composition," *Modern Philology* 56 (1959), 167–77.

Leavis, F.R. *The Great Tradition.* London: Chatto & Windus, 1948.

Long, Robert Emmet. "The Society and the Masks: *The Blithedale Romance* and *The Bostonians." Nineteenth-Century Fiction* 19 (1964), 105–22.

Lowenherz, Robert J. "The Beginning of 'Huckleberry Finn,' " *American Speech* 38 (1963), 196–201.

Lynn, Kenneth S. *Mark Twain and Southwestern Humor.* Boston: Little, Brown, and Co., 1959.

_____. *William Dean Howells: An American Life.* New York: Harcourt Brace Jovanovich. 1971.

Macnaughton, W. R. "The First-Person Narrators of Henry James," *Studies in American Fiction* 2 (1964), 145–64.

Marx, Leo. "The Pilot and the Passenger: Landscape Conventions and the Style of *Huckleberry Finn,"* *American Literature* 28 (1956). Rpt. in *Mark Twain: A Collection of Critical Essays.* Henry Nash Smith, ed. Englewood Cliffs, N.J.: Prentice-Hall, 1963, pp. 47–63.

_____. "The Vernacular Tradition in American Literature," in *Studies in American Culture.* Joseph J. Kwiat and Mary C. Turpie, eds. Minneapolis: University of Minnesota Press, 1960, pp. 109–22.

Matthiessen, F. O. *The James Family.* New York; Alfred A. Knopf, 1947.

Mayberry, George. "Reading and Writing," *New Republic* 7 May 1944, 608.

Melville, Herman. *Moby-Dick.* Harrison Hayford and Hershel Parker, eds. New York: W. W. Norton & Company, Inc., 1967.

Miller, Perry. *Nature's Nation.* Cambridge: Belknap Press of Harvard University Press, 1967.

Morrison, Sister Kristin. "James's and Lubbock's Differing Points of View," *Nineteenth-Century Fiction* 16 (1961), 245–55.

Page, Philip. "The Curious Narration of *The Bostonians,"* *American Literature* 46 (1974), 374–83.

Paine, Albert Bigelow. *Mark Twain: A Biography.* 3 vols. New York: Harper & Brothers, 1912.

Pederson, Lee. "Mark Twain's Missouri Dialects: Marion County Phonemics," *American Speech* 42 (1967), 261–78.

_____. "Negro Speech in the Adventures of Huckleberry Finn," *The Mark Twain Journal* 13, No. 1 (1965), 1–4.

Putt, S. Gorley. *Henry James: A Reader's Guide.* Ithaca: Cornell University Press, 1966.

"Realism Defined: William Dean Howells," in *Literary History of the United States: History.* R. E. Spiller, *et al.,* eds., 4th ed., rev. New York: Macmillan, 1974, pp. 878–98.

Rubin, Louis D., Jr. *The Teller in the Tale.* Seattle: University of Washington Press, 1967.

Rulon, Curt M. "Geographical Delimitation of the Dialect Areas in *The Adventures of Huckleberry Finn,*" *The Mark Twain Journal* 14, No. 1 (1967), 9–12.

_____. "The Dialects in *Huckleberry Finn.*" Ph.D. dissertation, University of Iowa, 1967.

Samuels, Charles Thomas. *The Ambiguity of Henry James.* Urbana: The University of Illinois Press, 1971.

Scott, Arthur L., "Introduction," in *Mark Twain: Selected Criticism.* Ed. with intro. by Arthur L. Scott. Dallas: Southern Methodist University Press, 1955.

Smith, Henry Nash. *Mark Twain: The Development of a Writer.* New York: Atheneum, 1967.

Stone, Albert E., Jr. *The Innocent Eye: Childhood in Mark Twain's Imagination.* New York: Archon Books, 1970.

Stone, William B. "Towards a Definition of Literary Realism," *Centrum* 1 (Spring, 1973), 47–60.

Tanner, Tony. *The Reign of Wonder: Naivety and Reality in American Literature.* New York: Harper & Row, Perennial Library, 1967.

Taylor, Gordon O. *The Passages of Thought: Psychological Representation in the American Novel, 1870–1900.* New York: Oxford University Press, 1969.

Terrie, Henry L., Jr. "Henry James and the 'Explosive Principle,' " *Nineteenth-Century Fiction* 15 (1961), 283–99.

Tilford, John E., Jr. "James the Old Intruder," *Modern Fiction Studies* 4 (1958), 157–60.

Trilling, Lionel. *The Opposing Self: Nine Essays in Criticism.* New York and London: Harcourt Brace Jovanovich, 1978.

Vanderbilt, Kermit. *The Achievement of William Dean Howells.* Princeton: Princeton University Press, 1968.

Yeazell, Ruth Bernard. *Language and Knowledge in the Late Novels of Henry James.* Chicago and London: The University of Chicago Press, 1976.

index